Japanese Manners & Ethics in Business

Japanese Manners & Ethics in Business

By
Boye De Mente

Phoenix Books/Publishers
Phoenix/Tokyo

Other Books by Boye De Mente

How to Do Business in Japan — A Guide for Foreign Businessmen
The Japanese as Consumers (With Fred Perry)
The Tourist & the Real Japan
Bachelor's Japan
Oriental Secrets of Graceful Living
Some Prefer Geisha / The Art of Mistress-Keeping in Japan
Faces of Japan / 23 Critical Essays
P's & Cues for Travelers in Japan
Businessman's After Hours Guide to Japan
Exotic Japan — The Traveler's Wonderland
Man's Guide to the Orient
Once A Fool — From Japan to Alaska by Amphibious Jeep
Face-Reading for Fun & Profit
Bachelor's Hawaii
Erotic Mexico — A Traveler's Unofficial Guide
Insider's Guide to Rocky Point, Nogales, Guaymas, Mazatlan & La Paz
Retiring in Arizona: Senior Citizen's Shangri La
Insider's Guide to Phoenix, Scottsdale, Tempe, Mesa & Tucson
Cookbook for Lovers
For Someone You Love — 15 Ways to Kick the Smoking Habit

Copyright (c) 1981 by Boye De Mente. All rights reserved. Published by PHOENIX BOOKS/Publishers, P.O. Box 32008, Phoenix, Arizona 85064 U.S.A.

Manufactured in the United States of America
Library of Congress Catalog Card Number: 75-3916.
ISBN: 0-914778-00-5

This book is dedicated to the memory of the late Ray A. Woodside and to my other friends in Japan, both foreign and Japanese, whose failures, successes, agonies and ecstasies are monuments to their courage and their efforts to work together, despite fundamental differences that often drive them to distraction.

Acknowledgements

I am deeply grateful to the following persons for reading the book when it was in manuscript form and making many suggestions for its improvement: James A. Henderson, Morry M. Iwashina, Frank H. Kawahara, and Earle T. Okumura. I am, however, solely responsible for its contents. — Boye De Mente.

Note from the Author

The original edition of this book came out in January, 1961. The publisher printed a modest 2,000 copies because he was afraid he might get stuck with them. The print-run was sold out within six weeks, and the book—slightly updated in 1965—went on to sell more than 50,000 copies.

This latest edition has been significantly revised—not because the manners and ethics of Japanese businessmen have changed that much in the intervening years, but to add to both the scope and depth of the contents, and hopefully make it even more useful.

There have, of course, been dramatic changes in Japan's world of business in the last several decades. But most of these changes have been superficial, with the underlying values and motivations remaining very much the same.

In fact, beginning in the early 1960s and continuing on into the 70s, there was a strong resurgence of faith in and commitment to the "pure" Japanese way of doing business among most of Japan's major corporations. In light of the reemergence of Japan as a great world power, it is difficult to find fault with the decision of Japanese businessmen to continue with—or in some cases, go back to—their traditional way of doing things.

An important consideration now, it seems to me, is how much Western businessmen might learn from the Japanese that would improve our own business system.

Boye De Mente
Tokyo

P.S.—Japanese words and phrases used in this book are followed by my own version of English-language phonetics. Just pronounce the phoneticized syllables as if they were standard English, and the words will come out in understandable "Japanese."

About the Author

Boye De Mente is the author of more than 15 books that have established him as an authority in such diverse fields as travel, aesthetics, entertainment and cross-cultural problems affecting Japanese-American business relations. Born in Missouri, Mr. De Mente spent the first 15 years of his adult life in the Far East, primarily in Japan and Hong Kong. He is a graduate of *Jochi University* in Tokyo and the *American Graduate School of International Management* in Glendale, Arizona.

Mr. De Mente began his career in the Far East in 1948 as a member of the Army Security Agency. From 1953 to 1962, with time out for a 4-month crossing of the Pacific Ocean in an amphibious jeep and some recuperating in Phoenix, Arizona, he served as a journalist and editor covering Japan, Korea, Taiwan, Hong Kong, Thailand and the Philippines.

Following the success of the first edition of this book (in 1961), De Mente "retired" from salaried employment and has averaged more than one book a year since. He is married to the former Margaret Warren of Tulare, California, and they have two daughters, Dawn and Demetra. The De Mentes make their home in Phoenix.

Contents

Chapter 1
Amae
"Indulgent Love" in Japanese Manners & Ethics

Amae	The "Oil" of Life in Japan 17
Shinyō	Trust in the Viscera 21
Uramu	That Hostile Feeling 22
Enryo	Looking at Things from a Distance 23
Giseisha	The Victim Mentality 24
Chokkan to Ronri	Intuition Vs. Logic 25
Koto to Shidai ni Yotte wa	Circumstantial Truth 26

Chapter 2
Tate Shakai
Living & Working in a Vertical Society

Oyabun-Kobun	Superiors & Subordinates 28
Sempai-Kōhai	Seniors & Juniors 31
Katagaki	Rank Means Everything 32
Meishi	Who Bows First? 33

Habatsu	Behavior by the Numbers 35
Gakubatsu	Rule by Cliques 37
Nenbatsu	Up by the Year 40
Shūdan Ishiki	All Together Now 42

Chapter 3
Wa
Peace & Harmony in an Up/Down World

Shintō	The Way of the Gods 43
Buddhism	The Way of the Bamboo 44
On	The Web That Binds 45
Sahō	Etiquette as Virtue 46
Giri	The Personal Code 50
Ninjō	Human Feelings 51
Kao wo Tateru	"Save My Face!" 51
Tsukiai	Paying Social Debts 52
Shōkaijō	A Short-Cut to Success 53
Hoshō-Nin	The Guarantor 56
Chukai-Sha	The In-Between Man 57
O'Miyage	Giving to the Cause 57
Mōshiwake Arimasen	Apology Without End 59
Ojigi	Politeness Makes Perfect 61
Kyōsō	Competition by the Numbers 64
Jichō	Staying Out of Trouble 65

Chapter 4
Kaisha
The Japanese Company

Uchi-no Kaisha	Companies as "Family-Clans" 66
Shikomu	Training in "Company Morality" 68
Shakai no Kurabu	The Company as a Social Club 69
Ichiryū, Niryū, Sanryū	1st Class, 2nd Class, 3rd Class 70
Jūyaku	"Big" Executives 72
Hako-no Naka Ni Hitobito	People in Boxes 73

CONTENTS 13

Bu	Finding the Right One 74
Bōnenkai	Meeting to Forget 77

Chapter 5
Manejimento
Aspects of Japanese Company Management

Shūshinkōyō	It's for Life! 80
Nenkō Jōretsu	The "Merit of Years" 82
Seishin	Training in Spirit 84
Onjō Shugi	"Mothering" Employees 85
Rinji-Saiyō	The Outsiders 86
Ringi Seido	Putting It in Writing 86
Nemawashi	Behind the Scenes 88
Kaigi	Talk Meets 89
Jūyaku ga Nai	No "Executives" in Japan 89
Hankō	Chopping People Down 90
Mibun	The Rights Have It 91
Hishō-kan	Where Are All the Secretaries? 94
Shigoto	It's Not the Slot 95
Tsūshin	Don't Call Me! 96
Yakusoku	On My Word 98
Sekininsha	Finding Where the Buck Stops 99
Mizu Shōbai	The "Water" Business 101

Chapter 6
Nippongo
The Magnificent Barrier

Japlish	Smooth as a Baby's Ass 105
Haji	Avoiding Shame 109
Sukoshi Dekimasu	I Can Do a Little 110
Wakarimasu ka?	Getting Through 112
Tsūyaku	"Thinking," Not Just Words 113
Gaijin Kusai	Smelling Like a Foreigner 115
Makoto	Sincerity, Japanese Style 117

Chapter 7
Yamato Damashii
The Spirit of Japan

Ware Ware Nippon-jin	"We Japanese" 120
Jibun ga Nai	Life Without a "Self" 121
Risshin Shusse	The Japanese Success-Drive 123
Ki ga Susumanai	100 Million Dissatisfied Spirits 125
Ichiban to Biri	Feeling Superior and Inferior 125
Mono-no Aware	Aesthetics in Business 129
Kanjō wo Sasuru	Emotional Strokes 131
Mōretsu Shain	The "Gung-Ho" Employees 132

Chapter 8
Matome
Summing Up

Humanism Plus Authoritarianism   135
The Parent-Child Ethic   136
"Marine Corps" Management   138
The Emotional-Sensual Element   139
The Kindness Syndrome   144
Sources of Japan's Strength   145
Pride, Prejudice & Perseverance   147

Chapter 9
Glossary of Useful & Interesting Terms

Amae
"Indulgent Love" in Japanese Manners & Ethics

Amae
The "Oil" of Life in Japan

The reader is invited to imagine a group of some 20 men and five women sitting on floor cushions behind low tables that have been arranged in the form of a hollow square in a huge Japanese-style room. The tables are covered with bowls, plates and various other dishes containing the leftovers of a meal. In front of each man is an unfinished bottle of beer or flask of *O'sake*. The five women are *Geisha*. While they keep up a steady patter of ribald banter with the men, they also see to it that nobody's beer glass or O'sake cup is empty.

Suddenly, one of the girls shouts, "How about a dance? Come on! Somebody dance!" Others take up the shout, calling out various names of men who are in the party. Finally, the man toward whom most of the shouts are directed stands up, arranges his *yukata* (you-cah-tah) robe and steps out into the center of the room. He slowly composes his face into an expressionless mask, assumes a formalized stance with his legs apart and, pulling a folded fan from his waist band, snaps it open with a flourish.

His audience claps loudly and roars its approval. One of the *Geisha* begins to pick out a slow, solemn tune on a *shamisen* (shah-me-sen). The man starts to dance. His audience quiets down and watches him in silence. He is grossly fat, with a stomach that bulges out in a ponderous blister. The flesh on his face has thickened and bloated his cheeks until his head is almost perfectly ball-shaped. His figure is grotesque in its misshapen stubbiness . . . but he dances beautifully; as graceful, if not as accomplished, as an 18-year old Geisha-trainee from Kyoto.

The dancer on our makeshift stage is the 55-year old president of a Japanese company that manufactures computer parts, and an ordinary businessman by Japanese standards. But when considered from a Western viewpoint, he is a bundle of complex contradictions.

In one area after another, it would seem that our typical Japanese businessman has only one thing in common with his Western counterpart—the desire to make money and prosper. But even this basic assumption does not always hold entirely true, so it is little wonder that Western businessmen often find themselves completely unable to understand or explain the attitudes or conduct of their Japanese colleagues.

Their methods of operating their businesses are different; their relationships with the people around them, employees and otherwise, are different; and, at least to some outward appearances, so are their motivations. They live and work by a set of rules—compounded from a unique culture—that are not only unknown to most foreigners but inherently alien to the average Westerner.

There have been tremendous changes in Japan since the country began intercourse with the West on a large scale. Some of the codes and manners of feudalistic Old Japan have withered away because they were completely incompatible with the new order. Others remain in only slightly weakened form to set the Japanese apart from all other people.

Not all of the characteristics that the Japanese inherited from their unique past are bad or disadvantageous by any means. Quite the contrary. But a number of them, especially as they manifest themselves in everyday business practices, are particularly difficult for the Westerner to understand, accept and appreciate.

The American especially, tends to become frustrated when dealing with his Japanese counterparts because our way of doing business happens to conflict more strongly and in more areas with many of the fundamental principles of the Japanese system.

Of course, the typical Japanese businessman is a product of the system he manifests, and to understand him one must know a great deal about the system. Furthermore, the foreign businessman resident in Japan as well as the executive who visits here must conform to some degree to the system. It is essential, therefore, that the foreign businessman know why the system exists and how it works.

In considering the Japanese from any viewpoint for any reason it is vital to remember that they are products of a unique civilization, that their standards and values are the results of several thousand years of powerful religious and metaphysical conditioning that were entirely different from those that molded the character, personality and habits of Westerners.

The most important differences resulting from the distinctive historical background of the Japanese are the social factors determining their character and personal relationships. The bedrock principles of the Japanese system, in business as well as in private life, are bound up in a number of special words which refer to a series of interrelated values, motivations, attitudes and practices forming the foundation of Japanese manners and ethics in business.

Which of these key words came first, or should come first, is somewhat arbitrary. I have chosen to begin with *amae* (ah-my) because it seems to me to be the pillar around which the traditional character, personality and aspirations of the Japanese are built.

Amae (ah-my) refers to what for lack of a better phrase in English is translated as "indulgent love"; the category or quality of love an infant feels for an absolutely kind and loving mother—and *must have from its mother to stay right with the world!*

The principle and practice of *amae* are certainly not unique to Japan, but the Japanese are apparently the only people (other than perhaps isolated tribes or islanders) who made it the primary essence of their distinctive social system.

In his authoritative book *Amae no Kozo* (Ah-my no Coe-zoe)—"The Structure of Amae"—published in English as *The Anatomy of Dependence*—Takeo Doi, one of Japan's leading psychiatrists, observes that while *amae* is the "oil of life" in Japan, the principle is generally unrecognized in the West, even though it is one of the fundamental building blocks of human (and animal!) personality.

In practical terms, the Japanese do not feel comfortable or "right" in any person-to-person relationship that does not include *amae*. By this, they mean a feeling of complete trust and confidence, not only that the other party will not take advantage of them, but also that they—businessmen *or* private individuals—can *presume upon the indulgence of the other.*

All people, says Doi, have a deep, innate desire to *amae*—to unload their troubles on someone they can trust, on someone from whom they can receive recognition and advice. In other words, we need someone who will relieve us of our excess psychic baggage.

In Doi's concept, it is the person who can "safely" encourage infantile dependence *(amae)* in its purest form who is most qualified to be elevated to a position of leadership in Japan. The leader, in being utterly dependent on those beneath him, is least likely to mislead them because he would be hurting himself.

The *amae* factor in Japanese psychology, according to Doi's line of reasoning, is what accounts for the "childish" behavior often ascribed to Japanese adults.

Expressed in another way, to *amae* (amaeru) means "to mother" and "to be mothered"—referring specifically to the purest form of ego-less relationship between a loving mother and an absolutely trusting infant. Without *amae* in infancy and childhood, notes Doi, the child's psyche and personality are scarred for life.

In Western societies, growing up has traditionally been related to *repressing* the need for *amae* and eventually giving up its practice—a factor that is obviously the key to some of the profound differences between Western and Japanese attitudes and behavior, since they emphasize *amae* throughout life.

Doi proposes that the *amae* mentality of the Japanese goes back to their primal experience during the dawn of their history. Futhermore, he adds, it was "national polity" until the beginning of the modern era. He says that the traditional Japanese concept of peace and harmony *(wa)*, which many older Japanese still feel Japan is obligated to spread to the rest of the world, is nothing more than "idealized *amae*."

Shinyō
Trust in the Viscera

Westerners have often commented on how difficult it is to develop a close personal relationship with a Japanese businessman, especially in a short period of time. Besides the communication and other cultural barriers that usually separate the two sides, the Japanese are reluctant to extend their friendship to anyone with whom they do not have *shinyō* (sheen-yoe)—trust, confidence, faith. To the Japanese, a man in whom they can have *shinyō* is a man of honor who will do what is expected of him whatever the cost.

The development of *shinyō* comes about only as a result of a successful *amae* relationship with another person; and this takes time—not weeks or months, but years. The foreign businessman who jets to Tokyo on a two or three year assignment—much less a short-term trip—cannot expect to establish close, personal ties with his Japanese colleagues that transcend either his foreignness or his professional role.

The *amae* relationship, involving the child-parent-adult personalities in each individual, is a kind of "game" the Japanese play in all walks of life, between subordinates and superiors, and sometimes between equals as well. Each individual has to know which role is proper for what situation, who can legitimately play that role, and how it should be played.

The foreign businessman in Japan, not being used to playing the parent role with employees (or the child role if he is approaching a senior Japanese businessman!), is usually unable to establish the kind of rapport the Japanese expect and feel comfortable with. As a result, there is almost always an under-current of tension in employee-management relations in Japanese/foreign firms, and in meetings between Japanese and Westerners.

By the same token, Japanese managers stationed abroad often find that they can no longer play the parent role smoothly even with Japanese subordinates working under them. The system simply doesn't work well outside the cultural context of Japan. Where foreign employees of overseas Japanese operations are concerned, the Japanese manager either keeps his distance or does his best to play the adult-to-adult role—an awkward situation at most because he usually has not had experience in adult-adult relationships with subordinates.

Uramu
That Hostile Feeling

When a subordinate's efforts to *amaeru* are ignored or rebuffed, he is deeply upset. In fact, Doi says that when a Japanese is unable to express his *amae*, the essential ingredient for the development of trust and faith in another person, a type of hostility called *uramu* (ou-rah-moo) emerges. This hostility, he explains, is manifested by a deep-seated feeling of resentment against the person or people (or whatever system) is involved.

Enryo
Holding Back

When the Japanese do not feel comfortable with someone or something—when they cannot practice *amae*—they practice *enryo* (in-ree-oh), literally, "considering (things) from a distance," a word you hear frequently in Japan, usually as *"Go-enryo-naku"* (go-in-ree-oh-nah-coo)—"Please don't be shy." Doi adds that while the individual Japanese themselves do not like to *enryo*, they expect others to do it. The Japanese *enryo* a great deal, however, because it is their customary way of opposing things or avoiding situations that might result in their incurring unwanted obligation, or in disrupting harmony.

In all relations with strangers, Japanese or foreign, business or private, the Japanese feel constrained to practice *enryo* excessively *because there are always barriers between people who do not have an amae relationship!*

Westerners generally do not—often cannot—verbalize the concept of *amae* the way the Japanese do because we do not have a specific, commonly known and used word for it. We are able to practice *amae* to a shallow but nevertheless important degree toward almost anyone, however; often immediately after meeting them. The Japanese on the other hand, either ignore strangers and the outside world or maintain a hostile stance toward them because their ability to feel and practice *amae* with others is based on long-term face-to-face relationships.

Earle Okumura* uses two variable concentrics (Figures 1 and 2, next page) to illustrate the basic differences in the psychology and personality of Japanese and Westerners.

Westerners, as shown in Figure 1, have a large, thick inner "core" (psyche), with a thin, easily penetrable outer "shell." The Japanese, on the other hand, (Figure 2), have a small, fragile inner core (psyche), with two outer "barriers" designed to keep people at a distance. The first barrier is

---

*Okumura is president of Okumura and Wilking, the Los Angeles-based consulting firm that specializes in acting as go-between for American and Japanese business interests.

thick and strong; the second one is conspicuously thin and fragmentary.

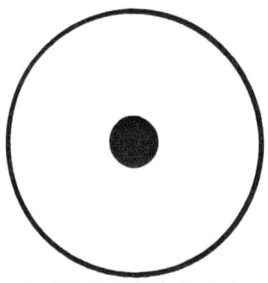

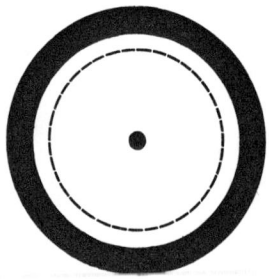

Figure 1 — Westerner   **Figure 2 — Japanese**

As the diagrams indicate, it is easy to approach a Westerner and get on relatively close terms in a short period of time—often within minutes. At the same time, however, the massive, solid "core" of the Westerner prevents the individual from really opening up, from dropping all barriers to the inner self. No matter how close Westerners may become, even husbands and wives, few of them can truthfully say they know the other person fully. There are invariably dark areas of doubt and wonder.

In contrast, the thick, outer barrier surrounding each Japanese makes it difficult and time-consuming to establish any kind of initial relationship. But once the heavy, protective guard is penetrated, the psyche of the Japanese is fully exposed—and extremely vulnerable to the unscrupulous person. The Japanese are therefore understandably wary of letting anyone inside their personal sphere.

Giseisha
The Victim Mentality

The Japanese, Doi continues, also suffer from an unusually strong, built-in susceptibility to injury as a result of their *amae* expectations—which give them an almost overwhelming tendency to become totally dependent on others. They experience this *giseisha* (ghee-say-e-sha) or "victim syndrome" anytime anybody or anything hinders or interferes with their aims or efforts. This feeling, he goes on, is most likely to be triggered when someone, some company or some country on which they have been passively dependent, does something they feel is against their interests.

This "victim mentality," Doi adds, also carries with it an underlying need to get revenge to wipe out the "insult."

Chokkan To Ronri
Intuition Vs. Logic

It is sometimes said that Japanese businessmen use *Jan-Ken-Pon* (Jahn-Kane-Pone) logic. *Jan-Ken-Pon* refers to the popular paper-scissors-stone game played with the hands and fingers by both young and old in Japan to settle questions or points of order. In this context it refers to logic that is cyclic, or elastic; not absolute.

In general terms, Japanese thinking tends to be intuitive instead of logical. Doi also explains this in terms of *amae*. He says the Japanese cultural characteristic of attempting to deny the fact of separation of mother and child, and to emotionally generate a sense of identity with nature, is fundamentally illogical.

Of course, intuitive thinking is not necessarily or always undesirable. The management philosophy followed by Konosuke Matsushita, founder of the huge Matsushita Electric (National-Panasonic) Corporation, and many of Japan's other most successful businessmen, is based on the use of intuitive intelligence.

Part of the intuitive process of this unique management philosophy is expressed in the term *kongen* (conegain), which means, more or less, "the root of the universe." It refers to the energy that fuels the universe—energy-wisdom that can be tapped by meditating; by emptying one's conscious mind of all thoughts, and thereby opening it to communication with cosmic consciousness. Matsushita, regarded by some as the greatest Japanese businessman of modern times, credited *kongen* with being the source of his management philosophy. Following his example, top Matsushita executives meditate regularly.

There are also many positive aspects to the practice of *amae*. It emphasizes tolerance, non-discrimination and equality. It also allows the Japanese to accept, absorb and assimilate non-threatening new ideas—technical, social or philosophical—without internal conflicts.

The deep, compelling urge the Japanese have to *amae* may also be responsible for the powerful lust they have for knowledge. Anything that is unfamiliar or unknown to them—therefore making an *amae* relationship impossible—represents an unacceptable threat. It is characteristic of the Japanese when faced with something new to say, "We must learn everything there is to know about it in order to protect ourselves—and if there is anything worthwhile in the new thing we will adapt it to our own uses."

Koto To Shidai Ni Wa
Circumstantial Truth

One of the first things that foreign commentators observed about the Japanese, beginning with Townsend Harris (America's first diplomatic representative in Japan), was their apparent disregard for the truth in the "Western" sense. Harris reported that they did not know the value of a straightforward and truthful policy and that they never hesitated to utter a falsehood when the truth would have served the same purpose.

Harris was regarded by the Japanese as a dangerous enemy agent, so it should not be surprising that an attempt was made to keep him in the dark. But many others who came after Harris reported the same thing, so it is important to look closely at the Japanese view and use of truth.

The "truth" in Japan has never been based solely on absolute principle, but has been expressed more in *amae* (read "human") terms as something that is relative and depends upon circumstances and obligations. Just as obligation and circumstance change, so does truth. A primary rule in traditional Japanese society was that nothing should be allowed to disrupt the surface serenity of existence. When a Japanese was asked a question, his natural impulse was to give an answer that would please the inquirer, even when it wasn't true. If he did not have a proper or plausible answer, he would answer in vague terms, or give no answer at all to avoid telling a lie.

Another aspect of truth in present-day Japan has to do with personal responsibility, decision-making and group orientation. The individual is often strictly limited in what he can say because he cannot act or pass judgments independently. This often puts a Japanese in a position of not being able to say anything about a certain matter.

The foregoing are not all of the ramifications of the *amae* principle in Japanese attitudes and behavior. The principle, one way or another, seems to touch on every aspect of Japanese life. Indeed, the structure of traditional Japanese society is believed by Doi and other social scientists to be an outgrowth of the dictates of *amae*. This social structure, to use the currently popular Japanese term, is a *Tate Shakai* (Tah-tay Shah-kie) or "Vertical Society."

Tate Shakai
Living & Working in a Vertical Society

Oyabun-Kobun
Superiors & Subordinates

With limited exceptions, human relations in Japan, particularly the formal and the professional, are based on "vertical" or superior/subordinate relationships between the people involved. There is, of course, nothing unusual about a society based on a hierarchical arrangement of inferiors and superiors. Most if not all societies are founded more or less on this structure. What makes Japan's "Vertical Society" different is that there is always one, single, distinctive relationship between individuals and between groups—or no relationship at all. It is the character of this relationship, or lack of relationship, that underlies not only the manners and ethics of Japanese businessmen, but most "Japanese" behavior.

The phrase "vertical society" was first used by Chie Nakane, professor of social anthropology at Tokyo University's Institute of Oriental Culture, in her fascinating book, *Tate Shakai no Ningen Kankei* (Tah-tay Shah-kie no Neen-gain Khan-kay-ee)—"Human Relations in a Vertical Society."

Professor Nakane sees the superior/subordinate structure of Japanese society, based on an "ego-centered" ranking, as the primary basis for social order in the country—not only shaping attitudes and behavior, but overshadowing everything else: character, personality, profession, ability and accomplishment.

If ranking, in a superior/inferior structure, is one side of the social coin in Japan, the other side is an equally deep and pervasive impulse among the Japanese to form themselves into and identify with groups on the basis of proximity and activity. Both ranking and grouping, as social and economic mechanisms, have their roots deep in Japan's culture. From ancient times, Japanese society was divided into distinct classes, clans and occupational groups. Each of these categories and all the members therein were ranked on a vertical scale beginning with the lowest laborer or retainer and going upward to the immediate master or boss, the village or town head, the clan lord and ultimately to the Emperor himself.

During Japan's Feudal Age (which did not end until 1868), these group affiliations were mostly hereditary and rigidly exclusive, which meant that for the most part an individual could better himself only within his own immediate group.

With the fall of the Feudal government in 1868 and the subsequent beginning of industrialization, both the clan and hereditary class systems were abolished. In the next few decades Japanese society underwent profound changes, with commercial enterprises and vast government bureaucracies replacing the economic as well as political functions of the traditional clans. In this new, open-ended situation, the basis for grouping and ranking individuals changed from status by birth-right to educational background and economic success in the marketplace. Neither the concept nor the mechanics of the vertical inferior/superior relationship between people was changed, however. It was simply transferred to the new bureaucratic and industrial order.

During Japan's long Feudal Age (1185–1868), this subordinate/superior principle was most often expressed in business contexts by the terms *Oyabun* (Oh-yah-boon) and *Kobun* (Coe-boon). *Oyabun* means "boss," "employer" or "master," and *kobun* means "employee," "follower" or "retainer." Shop, factory, and restaurant owners, the heads of construction gangs, political organizations and even criminal bosses were the *oyabun*. Their employees or followers were the *kobun*. *Oya* means "parent," while *ko* means "child," and is indicative of the connotation of these words.

From earliest times, the relationship between the *oyabun* and *kobun* was generally a long-term arrangement, often for life, and was intensely personal, incorporating elements of father-child, master-retainer and lord-slave in the relationship. Whatever the exact nature of the tie, each *oyabun-kobun* group functioned as a single unit, with the lives of the members and their families intimately linked together. The system thus had a stabilizing effect on society, politically as well as economically, and also acted as a very effective means of passing handicraft and business technology from one generation to the next.

In the *oyabun-kobun* system, advancement and authority were usually based on seniority first, and talent and accomplishment second. In a family-owned enterprise, succession was normally from father to son or son-in-law. But if the family heir was incompetent, the ranking employee ran the business.

While the system thus supported and protected the less able members of society, it tended to stifle the potential of those who had talent and ambition, and were not in line to succeed the master. Their only recourse was to break away from the group and start their own—not the easiest thing to do in Feudal Japan, when such behavior was frowned on.

The *oyabun-kobun* system is alive and well in Japan today, although not always officially described as such. In many shops and work groups—and hoodlum gangs—the boss is still deferentially referred to as *"Oyabun,"* and the employees and group members behave in the best *kobun*-manner. Period pictures in which the *oyabun-kobun* system is a prime feature are perenially popular fare among Japan's movie-going and TV-watching millions.

Sempai-Kōhai
Seniors and Juniors

In present-day Japan, the superior/subordinate relationship between individuals may be very conspicuous, or it may be so subtle it is difficult for an outsider to discern, much less appreciate. But it is there and is very powerful.

Today, the vertical, superior/subordinate concept is most often expressed in both business and educational situations by the terms *kōhai* (coe-hie) "junior" and *sempai* (semm-pie) "senior." There is a word for "equals" in the Japanese vocabulary, *dōryō* (doe-ree-oh), but it is seldom used because there is practically always something that makes one person inferior or superior to another. Equal business partnerships in Japan are, in fact, unusual because individuals who can function well together as equals are rare.

The basis for the *sempai-kōhai* relationship is educational and economic, plus a time factor. It is specifically related to schools attended, year of graduation, educational level achieved, where this experience took place in relation to any other specific individual, the organization one works for, longevity with the company, the size and importance of the company or organization, and the individual's title or grade.

While the superior/inferior relationship pertains specifically to individuals in the same school or same organization (and those who went to the same school and work for the same organization), the status that one gains from having attended a prestigious university and being employed by a leading company or government ministry, carries general social status as well; not to mention the higher income it guarantees.

Although the individual who was graduated from X school, works for Y company and has achieved a rank of Z on the managerial hierarchy is not obligated to behave as a subordinate in any chance contact with another individual whose school or firm outranks his own, he will most likely do so if the other person's superior "pedigree" becomes known.

The education/work-based, superior/inferior system in Japan thus touches every individual in the country one way or another. Even the individual from a wealthy, "name" family is nominally inferior to his senior classmates in school and to his senior colleagues at work later. Even if the company is family-owned he must behave in the manner prescribed for subordinates.

Kata-Gaki
Ranks Means Everything

The key to Japan's superior/subordinate structured system is *Kata-gaki* (Cah-tah-gah-key) or "ranking." Everything and everybody is ranked, within whatever school they attend or organization they work for, first on the basis of their educational background, then their seniority, and finally on personality, talent and ability to get along with others.

In the business world, as well as a number of the professions, the specific rank of individuals (who have rank) is expressed in titles that usually end in the suffix *chō* (choe), which means "leader" or "chief." Over and above these obvious symbols of rank is the status of the company or other organization in which the individual has rank—if the place of employment is a well-known one of which the worker is proud. This status is visually exhibited by the company lapel button worn by employees of most major corporations.

Meishi
Who Bows First?

Relative rank between individuals in particular enterprises and organizations, and to a lesser extent between them and outsiders, determines not only the behavior, but the rights, privileges, responsibilities and obligations of the individual Japanese. It is therefore very important to every Japanese businessman that he know the rank of everyone with whom he comes into contact. He must know not only the personal rank of any individual concerned, but also the rating of his employing organization. One consideration here is that a section chief in a large, powerful company "outranks" a department head from a smaller, less important company.

This vital need to know the other's rank is the reason for the universal use and importance of the *meishi* (may-ee-she) or "name-card" in business in Japan. The card tells the receiver the rank of the individual and something about the stature of the company he represents.

After receiving an individual's card (with both hands and while bowing slightly), each recipient takes several seconds to look closely at the name of the other person's company, its address, and his title, before beginning any conversation. Besides revealing which of the two persons is subordinate to the other, and thus establishing the level of language each will use, name-cards often reveal common areas that can be quickly utilized to strengthen the new relationship—office addresses in the same area, a relative who works for the other company or a subsidiary, and other such personal links.

Foreign businessmen doing business with the Japanese should be aware of the function and importance of the name-card, and know how to use it. Because of its particular function, there is a prescribed manner for exchanging name-cards. The card must be presented while the very first stages of the introduction are taking place, so the Japanese recipient will be able to determine your rank and thus know how to respond to you.

The normal procedure is for the Japanese to hand you his name-card and accept yours at the same time, read your card and then formally greet you—traditionally by bowing and making appropriate remarks. This process is naturally facilitated if one side of your name-card includes Japanese translations of your name, title and company—and of course you should present your card "Japanese side" up.

It is surprising how many foreign businessmen go to Japan, or greet Japanese visitors in their own offices, without having name-cards printed in Japanese. It is not a matter of courtesy. It is a reflection of your business sense, your personal image of yourself and your company, your attitude toward Japan, and more.

Besides the role of the name-card itself often being misunderstood and misused by uninitiated foreign businessmen, the Western habit of immediately shaking hands upon being introduced to someone also frequently messes up meetings with Japanese. Since the handshake is a formal greeting in itself, this reverses the procedure as far as the Japanese are concerned.

While not too serious, especially if the handshake is quickly followed up by the presentation of name-cards, this is an area where the foreign businessman *can* extend a little courtesy by presenting his card before shaking hands.

As a result of the Vertical Society, rank pervades the lives of Japanese businessmen, wherever they may be. They joke among themselves that when they play golf, it is customary to tee off in accordance with the size of their salaries (it used to be the capital of their companies).

In any meeting, the Japanese businessman is bound by the rules of the senior/junior ranking system, and by the additional necessity of maintaining harmony. What he says, how he says it, and when he says it is determined by his rank within the group.

Another graphic indication of the attention paid to status is the common practice of making careful arrangements to seat individuals according to their rank at formal dinner parties and other official functions.

Habatsu
Behavior by the Numbers

For all of the cohesiveness and sameness exhibited by Japanese society when viewed from the outside, the Japanese are in fact splintered into big and little groups, economically, socially and politically, with the various groups revolving around individual companies, government ministries, hospitals, schools and sundry organizations. These thousands of separate groups are of vital importance because by opening or closing their doors to individuals, they hold the keys to success for the overwhelming majority.

Success, for all except the rare individual in Japan, is getting into the "right" group. The individual can generally get into one of these choice vertically structured groups only at the bottom, when he or she is young and just out of school. The most conspicuous exceptions have traditionally been retiring high-level government bureaucrats who are regularly taken into industry on executive levels because of the value of the influence they retain with their former, junior colleagues in their old bureaus. This practice is commonly referred to as *Amakudari* (Ah-mah-coo-dah-ree) or "Descending from Heaven"—the implication being, of course, that giving up the power, prestige, security and harmony of a vice minister's post for the rough uncertainty of the commercial world is a considerable step down.

Another, newer exception to the long established custom of bringing in new employees or group members only at the bottom is called *Chūto Saiyō* (choo-toe sie-yoe), which means "Mid-Career Appointment." Beginning in about 1970, it became expedient for many companies to go outside their "closed system" to occasionally hire middle-aged, experienced personnel with needed technical expertise; thus "mid-career" recruitment.

Not surprisingly, employees in the *Chūto Saiyō* category may not be treated like "regular" employees. Their pay is usually one or two steps below that being received by regular employees in their own age group (because to pay them the same would be "unfair" to the employees who had been with the company all their working lives), and they are often discriminated against in various other, more subtle ways.

Despite the *Amakudari* and *Chūto Saiyō* exceptions where major enterprises (but not government jobs) are concerned, most desirable companies are still basically closed to the entry of outsiders except by young people just out of school who come in at the bottom of the pyramid. Once an individual has become a member of a large company or elite organization, and has spent considerable time there, it becomes either difficult or impossible for him to become a fully accepted member of another organization.

There are several reasons for this. In a system in which promotion, income, prestige, etc., are primarily based on seniority, a new member coming in anywhere except at the bottom (or the very top) breaks the "chain" and throws everyone directly below the new member off schedule for life.

When a Japanese quits a large company (any company!) and moves to another one—something that is still rare by American standards—he cannot take his personal connections and good relations with him. Generally speaking, he will never be able to develop the same relationships over again with his new co-workers. Japanese managers who have switched employers and spent more than 10 years with their new companies frequently report that they are still regarded as "outsiders."

Quitting a large, well-known company and going to another one—or being transferred by a parent company to a distant subsidiary or a young joint-venture—is therefore a serious proposition for a Japanese manager, because it means he has been cast adrift from the ties that mean the most to him.

Since both the grouping and advancement-by-seniority systems in Japan put everything on a personal basis, close human relations are the "cement" of Japanese society, in business as well as private life. One company will not do business with another company until the managers who would be involved in initiating and continuing the business relationship have developed personal relations to the extent that they can satisfactorily *amaeru* with each other. This process of developing the necessary personal relations before establishing business ties with a new company is prescribed, meticulous and time-consuming.

Gakubatsu
Rule by Cliques

As in all countries, Japan's institutions of higher learning are ranked, unofficially, by various standards—age, origin, size, wealth, reputation of the staff and facilities, their political and economic influence. Most important for the ambitious young man in Japan, they are also ranked on the basis of the career job opportunities almost completely reserved for graduates of the top universities.

In the early years of Japan's modernization, top government posts and choice managerial positions naturally went to graduates of the first universities—some of which were government-sponsored. As the years passed and other universities appeared, graduates of the oldest institutions continued to monopolize the best jobs in the country simply because they were favored by their alumni brothers who occupied top positions in most leading government ministries and companies.

This practice was inevitably categorized under the term *gakubatsu* (gah-coo-baht-sue), which means something like "school cliques." While informal, these cliques, each one pertaining to the graduates of a specific, elite university, continue to dominate top posts in government and in many commercial enterprises.

Tokyo Daigaku (Die-gah-coo) or Tokyo University (*Todai* for short) is at the apex of Japan's educational pyramid. Hundreds of young men and women impair their health and bring great mental suffering on themselves and their families each year in their attempts to pass the entrance examinations with a high enough score to get into *Todai*. Almost every year there is at least one student who commits suicide because of repeated failures to win admittance.

Japan's young know only too well that if they do not get into *Todai* they are probably forever barred from several top-ranking companies and ministries because these institutions hire mostly *Todai* graduates. By the same token, those who succeed in getting into Tokyo University know they have it made for the rest of their lives. It often seems, in fact, that it doesn't make too much difference whether or not they learn anything, just as long as they get in and graduate.

"The road to *Todai* begins from kindergarten," a Japanese saying goes, by way of describing how difficult it is for a student to get into the university. Competition is so fierce that by the early 1960s it had spread down to the kindergarten level—a certain number of them graduating more students who eventually succeeded in passing the entrance exams to *Todai*.

Japanese universities hold entrance examinations once a year. If a student taking the exam fails, in competition with all the others taking the same examination, he has to wait a full year before trying to get into the same university again. High school graduates who fail to get into the university of their choice, and opt to wait until the following year to try again, rather than take the examinations to a less desirable university, are popularly called *ronin*, literally "wave men," the old term for *Samurai* warriors who had no master and roamed the country (often causing trouble).

In the case of Tokyo University, for every student who passes the entrance exams on the first attempt, several dozen fail and become *ronin*. Many who have gotten this far refuse to give up without a long struggle, and go back year after year in the hope that they will make it the next time. Others, deciding that the odds against them are too great, give up and settle for a second or third-choice university.

A similar situation exists, to a lesser degree, for several universities ranked immediately below Todai—*Keio* (Kay-oh), *Waseda*, (Wah-say-dah), *Kyoto University*, *Hitotsubashi*, (He-tote-sue-bah-she), *Kobe University*, etc. Like *Todai*, they enjoy the special "patronage" of certain enterprises and government bureaus.

There is a special word used when referring to the "job-getting success" of graduates of specific high schools and universities: *shushokuritsu* (shu-show-coo-ree-t'sue)—which means the "rate of employed versus number of graduates." In other words, the percentage of graduates from a particular school who succeed in getting jobs with desirable companies or government ministries determines the school's *shushokuritsu*—the "job-getting success" of its students.

Sports activities are very popular and important in Japanese universities because leading companies like to hire well-known athletes. There is usually a club for each sport. Among club members, the *sempai-kōhai* (senior-junior) syndrome reigns supreme, with emphasis on proper behavior of juniors toward seniors—who are sometimes referred to as *Dai-Sempai* (Die-Semm-pie) or "Great Seniors." "Proper behavior" is based on the concept of complete subordination.

Occasionally, a *Dai-Sempai* who is a graduate of a particular university and is in a responsible position in a prestigious company will accept an invitation from his old sports club to visit its summer training camp. There, both school and club ties are reaffirmed, and it is made explicit that the *Dai-Sempai* will do all he can to help members of the club get into his company after they graduate.

Such relationships, established on a hot summer day on the playing field, are cherished for a life-time by students who end up being employed by the company concerned, and serve as a significant factor in major personnel decisions by leading Japanese companies.

Many of the elite universities set certain standards, such as the number of A's an individual earns during the senior year, to determine whether or not the student gets a recommendation from his professor to a desirable company.

University students in their senior year also compete for the privilege of doing their theses under the direction of the most popular professors, who are often retained as consultants by leading enterprises and therefore have strong connections with the personnel departments of these companies. Each professor conducts a "thesis seminar" for 15 to 20 students, helping them select topics and guiding them in their research and writing.

Western executives serving in Japan who are recognized authorities in certain business fields might benefit themselves and their firms by offering to act as free advisers to these "thesis seminars." By establishing such a relationship with the university, with individual professors and graduating students, the executives would come into contact with outstanding young men and women looking for career opportunities.

"Nenbatsu"
Up by the Year

Besides the *gakubatsu* or "school clique" factor in the headier heights of Japan's business and professional world, there may also be "Year-Clubs" in certain ministries and in some major firms. A "year-club" is a grouping of all the new university graduates who entered the company or ministry the same year—regardless of what university they graduated from.

As members of a particular year-club accrue seniority in the organization, they look out for each other. Their entry-year loyalty may be so strong they avoid developing close relationships with other co-workers—including those from the same university but from different graduating classes. Members of the same year-club expect to be promoted at the same time and thus move up the executive escalator together. Even when new employees do not formally align themselves in such "clubs," they still expect to go up in unison.

Some Japanese critics blame the year-clubs and advancement-by-seniority for an "excess" of assistant managers and managers in the typical Japanese company. But the larger and older the company, the deeper the systems are likely to be entrenched. The trend in the past has been for new companies and rapidly growing smaller companies to start out with a merit system, or at least a partial merit system, for pay and promotion purposes. But in all cases so far, the passing of time has seen the appearance—sometimes gradual and sometimes sudden—of the seniority system. The Japanese, say the country's businessmen-philosophers, like the security of it.

Because success in Japan is so intimately tied to educational level, as well as to the prestige of the university attended, and because the highest ranking universities have been more or less sanctified as a result of their exalted role in the nation's life, the situation provides the foreigner with a way to get partially inside Japanese society. I say "partly" because no foreigner has ever gotten all the way inside Japanese society, and is not likely to in the foreseeable future.

This "way" consists of attending and graduating from one of the better known and respected Japanese universities. Not only will the ties with your Japanese classmates approximate those among themselves, you are also accorded a certain amount of respect and acceptance by Japanese who graduated before you did, as well as by those who come after you. Attending school together in Japan is very much like becoming a blood-brother in the American Indian sense.

Shudan Ishiki
All Together Now

Most top Japanese businessmen tend to be businessmen/philosophers, very much concerned with the ethics and morality of the Japanese enterprise system, and its perpetuation. One of the ways they attempt to achieve their purpose is to promote a type of group-thinking called *shūdan ishiki* (shu-dahn ee-she-key). This way of thinking emphasizes the functions and goals of the group, as opposed to thinking in terms of the experience, qualifications and responsibilities of the individual.

The *shūdan ishiki* type of thinking has, of course, long been an ideal of Japanese society.

Chapter 3

Wa
Peace & Harmony in an Up/Down World

Shintō
The Way of the Gods

No society, whatever its structure, can remain viable very long without explicit rules and restrictions governing the behavior of its members. For Japan's "vertical society," these guidelines were based on principles incorporated in, among others, the words *wa* (wah), *Ninjō* (neen-joe), *on* (own), *giri* (ghee-ree) and *tsukiai* (tsue-key-aye).

Wa, which may be translated as "peace and harmony," is one of the most important words in the vocabulary of Japan. The Japanese concept of peace and tranquility (in behavior as well as thought) is implicit in the concept of *amae*, or indulgent love, described earlier, and may have originated in *Shintō*, the native religion of Japan.

Shintō (Sheen-toe)—The Way of the Gods—is an ancient body of beliefs, without a bible or other written works, which tells the Japanese that they are the descendants of a group of heavenly beings, that all men and all things are spiritual brothers, that both spiritual and physical harmony is necessary to keep man and things right with the cosmos.

The *Shintō* concept that is most explicit in Japan's management philosophy is belief in *musubi* (moo-sue-bee), or "the undifferentiated co-existence of men, nature and the gods." Translated into practical terms, Japanese businessmen believe that spiritual unity should be the foundation for all relations between management and employees.

The Way of the Gods teaches that every man is his brother's keeper, and that to achieve and practice *amae* all men must be selfless. Of course, there were contradictions in the social structure of the Japanese right from the very beginning, with those descended from "superior deities" being superior beings, but in the main, *Shintōism* resulted in the majority of the Japanese, until modern times, being strongly influenced by the concept of "instinctive unselfishness" and harmonious behavior.

In any event, the concept of *wa* has been repeatedly designated throughout Japan's history as the foundation of the country's Imperial system and the ideal for which all Japanese should strive. Still today, the word *wa* is forever on the tongues of politician, statesman and businessman alike as they exhort their fellow countrymen to control themselves and to set an example for the world. There is in fact an old Japanese belief that they were divinely ordained to spread Japanese *wa* to the rest of the world.

Buddhism
The Way of the Bamboo

Much of the passivity and "bending with the bamboo" associated with Japanese manners and attitudes is attributed to *Buddhism*, which was introduced into Japan in the 6th century A.D., and has since co-existed with *Shintōism* as well as various aspects of *Confucianism*.

While there are many facets of *Buddhism*, a basic tenet is co-existence of man and nature, and non-violence. The practicalities of life, however, led the Japanese to develop such concepts as passive resistance to get one's way, "losing to win," and *jujitsu* (jew-jeet-sue), the martial art that turns an opponent's strength and aggressiveness into a weapon against him.

Confucianism, the third religious ethic that played a vital role in the shaping and coloring of Japanese culture, was primarily responsible for the philosophy—loyalty to one's superiors—that justified, and controlled, the superior/subordinate vertical structure of the society.

On
The Web That Binds

Within the context of the traditional Japanese social system and its emphasis on *wa*, the key word was *on* (own), which refers to the various obligations—to themselves, to each other, to their clan or country, and to the world—that all Japanese were automatically "assigned" at birth, or that they incurred during their lifetime.

These various obligations, all designed to maintain peace and harmony within the confines of the superior/inferior "vertical" system, formed the principles on which Japan's extraordinary society grew—a society that was built upon a class and ranking system in which position, severely prescribed manners, rights and responsibilities were absolute values that were imposed upon the people with relentless power.

As long as they remained members of their society, the Japanese of pre-industrial Japan were not free to say anything, take any action, in fact have any thought, that was not prescribed by the dictates of their position and by the *on* adhering to that position. A Japanese could not (and still cannot!) even say "sit down" without using words that properly denoted his position in life in relation to the person addressed. In bowing, a Japanese had to know not only when to bow but how low to bow and how many times.

Sahō
Etiquette as Virtue

It is difficult for the Western mind to grasp just how important these manners were to the early Japanese. Westerners are generally conditioned to conduct their lives according to certain abstract principles, with manners playing only a minor role. In Japan, the emphasis was reversed and a social system was forged in which the ultimate virtue was a prescribed conduct. Morality as it is known in the West was an aspect of manners.

From around the 6th century A.D. to the beginning of the modern era in 1868, the Japanese were more concerned with form than sincerity or accomplishment. The people were required to walk a certain way, to move their hands in a certain way, to open doors a certain way, to sleep with their head pointing in a certain direction and with their legs arranged in a certain way. The style and manner of their dress was prescribed by law for several generations before the beginning of the modern era. Their manner of eating was severely prescribed, they could enter a house only a certain way, greet each other only a certain way. Even physical movements necessary to perform many types of work were definitively established and no deviation was allowed.

So rigid and so severe were these prescribed manners that they long ago became a part of the Japanese personality—permeating and shaping every phase and facet of their lives, and passed on from one generation to the next. Most foreign businessmen dealing with Japan soon learn that still today there is a "Japanese Way" to do everything as a result of this meticulous conditioning.

Japan's Feudal Age is full of amazing and sometimes shocking incidents of what happened to people who behaved in an "other than expected manner." One of the most quoted of these incidents involved a farmer named Sogo who went over the head of his local lord to complain of starvation taxes to Japan's military dictator *(Shogun)*. For having broken a rule of conduct, Sogo was forced to watch while his three small sons were beheaded. Then he and his wife were crucified—although his complaint proved justified and the local lord was later removed from office.

Japanese society was therefore utterly cruel in that a man's morals were *visible for all to see*. For many centuries, a serious breach of etiquette in Japan was just as much a crime as murder or robbery is in the West. And the broken rule of conduct that made the death penalty inevitable did not have to be very important from our point of view.

Until well after the middle of the last century it was legal for a *Samurai*, the sword-carrying, privileged ruling class of Japan, to immediately kill any common individual who failed to show him proper respect—and a disproportionate number of the *Samurai* were among the most arrogant and status-conscious men that have ever lived.

Perhaps worse than this was the fact that whenever a Japanese failed to live up to his obligations or was remiss in his manners toward anyone of importance, he lost his place in life. This, still today, is an important consideration in the lives of the Japanese.

Not only class, but sex, age, family ties, and previous dealings also determined the behavior of the Japanese in every aspect of their lives. Form and manner—the outward expressions of the system—were sanctified as virtues. The extent to which this stratified and categorized society developed in Japan would be unbelievable if it were not for the fact that it still flourishes today, especially in the professional and business world, in only slightly diluted form.

Business as well as all other relations in Japan have traditionally been conducted within the web of this etiquette system, based on personal obligations owed to others. All dealings, public and private, were (and still are to a great extent) conducted within a set of rules that were designed to prevent trouble, to prevent or control change. Japan's *Golden Rule* was perfect hierarchal harmony at any human cost!

It was the law for many decades that in case of quarrels or fights among the people both sides would be equally punished without inquiry into the cause of the fight and regardless of whether one party was completely innocent. This discouraged public squabbles of any kind among the people, and so deeply embedded the habit of public harmony in the Japanese that up to about 1950, one could live in Japan for years without ever seeing or hearing a public row.

If someone stepped on another's toes or had an accident, the persons involved bowed to each other, mumbled a series of polite expressions and went on their way—or very quietly exchanged name-cards if the incident was serious. Even taxi drivers adhered to this rigid principle of formal politeness until as late as the mid-1950s. People seldom raised their voices in anger and it was even rarer for one person to strike another in public.

In order to guarantee conformity to such strict rules, it was necessary for Japan's Feudal Government to make use of an Orwellian system of control and punishment. Like the inhabitants of George Orwell's *1984*, but pre-dating it by several centuries, the Japanese of Feudal Japan were supposed to watch their family, friends and neighbors and report all infractions of rules to the proper authorities—often with disastrous results for those reported.

The control system in Feudal Japan was in fact more encompassing and more cruelly enforced than Orwell's futuristic nightmare. At least in Orwell's world it was kept on an individual basis, but in Japan the Feudal authorities held a man's family and sometimes his neighbors or even his whole village responsible for his actions. If he broke a regulation, the whole group was liable for punishment. Instances in which a whole family was destroyed or a clan broken up for the transgressions of one person are a compelling part of Japanese history.

The businessman in Japan today reflects the results of these centuries of conditioning in harmony in many ways: his dread of personal responsibility; his preference for mutual cooperation and group effort; his tendency to follow the mass and to imitate success; his reluctance to openly oppose anyone; his desire to submerge his individualism into his surroundings, etc. As a result of this conditioning, he is and has been for over a thousand years the nearly perfect Organization Man.

A further result of the enforcement of Japan's *Golden Rule* of *Wa* and a factor that makes it possible to generalize about Japanese businessmen with an astonishing degree of accuracy, is their mental homogeneity. As early as the 10th century, Japanese society had already developed into a "highly specialized, intense and uniform civilization" in which the people dressed the same—within their class—ate the same foods, were subjected to the same experiences, had the same stock of knowledge and the same prejudices. This sameness was so pervasive that, according to cultural historians, ordinary means of communication were unnecessary. The Japanese were so attuned to each other's attitudes and manners that the slightest hint or gesture was sufficient to convey their meaning with an almost magical facility.

It is not hard to understand the reasons for this extraordinary similarity of the Japanese. First, there was nearly complete isolation from the rest of the world for the first several thousand years of the country's human history. Second, the restricted area of the islands resulted in all the various influences that shaped the culture being felt at about the same time and more or less evenly by all the people.

Jesse F. Steiner, describing Japan before the Pacific War (1941–1945) was more matter-of-fact in his analysis of this characteristic.* He pointed out that the Japanese should be easy to understand because their lives for centuries had been governed by stereotyped conventions and a rigid social code. There was, he notes, an appropriate behavior for every situation, and a prescribed form to be followed for every action of life, both public and private.

---

*Steiner, Jesse F., *Behind the Japanese Mask*, The MacMillan Company, New York, 1943

Giri
The Personal Code

While *on* may be said to be the "universal" obligations the Japanese accrue as a result of being born, raised, educated and employed, *giri* (ghee-ree) is the personal code, the deep sense of duty, of honor, that compels them to fulfill their obligations—for good or bad.

Both *on* and *giri* are reciprocal in nature, and derive from a relationship in which the subordinate is expected to extend service and loyalty to the superior, and the superior is obligated to demonstrate responsibility and gratitude to the subordinate. Without *giri*, the *on* system would disintegrate.

This code of honor is often referred to as "*giri* to one's name." Failure to keep *giri* to one's name results in loss of "face." Westerners are of course familiar with the idea of "losing face" as the term has been applied to Japanese and other Asians. The idea and the words have been bandied about since before the turn of the century. But few appreciate the significance of the terms or how important the idea of *face* is to everyday business and social life in Japan. To "lose face" means much more to a Japanese than being embarrassed or insulted means to others, except in the very strongest sense of the words.

Although such great sensitivity to all outside influences is a tremendous handicap for the Japanese, it is not something they can take off like a coat. It is a part of their national character. It is especially important for people who have professional status of any kind or degree to protect their face. Maintaining their face or reputation as a professional person does not mean, however, that they have to be skilled in their line of work or conduct themselves ethically. It means, instead, that they cannot, in *giri* to their name, admit ignorance or inability, or allow anyone to besmirch their name, without serious consequences to their self-image and sense of well-being.

Ninjō
Human Feelings

But *giri* without human guidelines would have been unthinkable for the Japanese. These were provided by other principles within the framework of appropriate *ninjō* (neen-joe), or human feelings. One of the first things even the casual observer in Japan learns is that the Japanese measure, or try to measure, everything in terms of "human feelings." Their business system, they say, respects human feelings—while most other business systems "do not."

In short, it is typical Japanese ethics and behavior to give precedence to human feelings in most situations where possible, including many occasions when objective-thinking Western businessmen would unhesitatingly give precedence to profit considerations or other such "non-human" factors.

Many of the aspects of doing business in Japan that baffle or frustrate Western businessmen can only be understood in terms of *ninjō*.

Kao Wo Tateru
"Save My Face!"

Most "old-fashioned" Japanese businessmen still believe it is the height of rudeness to come out in the open and state opinions or unpleasant truths frankly because there is the possibility of loss of face. Whereas Americans, especially, are in the habit of "laying all their cards on the table," the Japanese have been conditioned to speak vaguely, and when necessary to resort to circumlocutions rather than make a frank statement that might give offense. This basic difference in attitudes and manners puts both Japanese and Westerners at a disadvantage when they are dealing with each other. The Western businessman too often assumes that his openness is being reciprocated, and it may be too late to rectify matters when he discovers his mistake.

Japanese firms also have a particularly sensitive "face" that must be maintained. In pre-modern days, this concept was often expressed by using the term *noren* (no-rain), which in its original meaning refers to the short, split curtains the Japanese have been hanging across the doors of shops and restaurants for centuries. The *noren* are usually made of navy blue cloth and bear the name or crest of the owner. In the early days *noren* came to embody the "face" of the business concerned, and business owners zealously guarded their symbol.

Eventually it became customary for the owners of established *noren* to allow one of their employees—the oldest one, the favorite, or one who had married into the owner's family—to go out and set up his own business, using the symbol (trademark) of his former employer; thus becoming a "branch" of the original house. In this way, a number of businesses gradually formed a network of closely affiliated stores spread out over wide areas.

Many of the *noren* famous in Japan today go back several hundred years and in some cases the owners of famous ones "rent" them out. The well-known Fuji Bank does business under the symbol of the Yasuda family, one of Japan's most respected *Zaibatsu*. Present-day businessmen value their company face just as highly as did their predecessors. It is common—especially in Osaka—to hear a businessman say he will not (or cannot) do something because of respect he must pay to his "face," or because it might "scar" his company's "face." Still, the Japanese are always being forced to put their face on the line for one reason or another, and therefore make frequent use of the phrase, *"Kao wo tatette kudasai"*—"Please save my face!"

Tsukiai
Paying Social Debts

The Japanese are naturally sensitive to incurring new obligations arbitrarily because there are so many they can't avoid, and because discharging their normal obligations is such a heavy burden. Honoring the obligations that develop between individuals who have a special relationship —not always a happy or pleasant duty—is more often than not done simply to maintain friendly relations—for the sake of *tsukiai* (t'sue-key-eye) as the Japanese so commonly say.

In practical terms, *tsukiai* refers to the social debt the student owes his professor, the employee owes his employer, the politician owes his patron, or that anybody owes to anyone who does them a favor, especially of a vital nature whose effects are continuous over an extended period of time. To "have *tsukiai*" with someone—be obligated to them—is an important social and economic factor in Japan.

All Japanese are under strong pressure to practice *tsukiai* by honoring their social debts. Failure to do so is a serious transgression if the occasion is an appropriate one —such as when a professor seeks a favor from a former student now occupying a high position in some company or government office.

Shōkaijō
A Short-Cut to Success

In business, the *tsukiai* factor is often used in the form of the *shōkaijō* (show-kie-joe) or "introduction," a very important ingredient in Japanese manners and ethics in business.

Westerners are, of course, familiar with the practice of giving and receiving introductions in the regular conduct of their business. But the system, especially as used in the U.S., doesn't compare with the role of the *shōkaijō* in Japan. Americans are not compelled by generations of conditioning and centuries of tradition to treat an introduction as anything more than mere politeness. The American businessman on the receiving end of an introduction can politely turn the caller away or decline to take any action on his behalf without fearing that his relationship with the man who gave the introduction will suffer. Not so the Japanese; particularly if the introduction is from a valued friend, a superior or an important business contact.

The businessman who is most susceptible to an introduction is the man most concerned with maintaining his "face" among those to whom he owes *tsukiai*.

The *shokaijo* itself is an institutionalized factor in Japan, with wide ramifications that touch on many aspects of daily life. It owes its role and power to several things, from the exclusivity and wariness toward outsiders that is inherent in the vertically structured group system; to the desire of the Japanese not to lose face for any reason; to the principle of group responsibility; and to their tendency to avoid personal involvement with outsiders or strangers.

The least that can be said is that in Japan it is considered rude to approach someone directly, without an introduction from a mutual friend or business contact. If you go through proper channels—an introduction—it shifts responsibility to the third party. The Japanese tend to be suspicious of anyone who approaches them without an introduction, and most Japanese would not think of making such an approach.

There are several types of introductions commonly used by the Japanese when they want to meet someone for business purposes. The most common one is from someone to whom the person you want to meet is personally obligated—one of his superiors; and old university professor; someone who has helped his family; a close relative or personal friend. Another popular type of introduction is one from a senior executive in a company with which the person you want to meet has substantial business obligations, such as from the vice president of a bank where he has made a loan, or from an important buyer or supplier.

Less effective but still useful is an introduction from a senior officer in a company with which the individual's firm has business relations. A non-personal introduction from a well-known bank, company or other known organization is probably the weakest of the introductions but is better than none. The foreign executive planning on doing business in Japan, or already in business there, certainly should make an effort to obtain introductions to any individual or company he wants to approach.

While the best introduction is a personal one to an individual, the foreign businessman will generally find that he cannot rely *only* on an approach to a single individual in a Japanese company. To be successful, any approach must also take into consideration all other sections and departments that are concerned.

Again, while there is only one "right" way to meet a Japanese businessman, and that is through an introduction, the Japanese regularly make exceptions to this where foreigners are concerned. In fact, foreigners who show up at Japanese companies without either appointments or introductions are often shown into the office of the highest executive available. This is usually no more than "Japanese politeness" and cannot be taken as a sign of interest in the caller or his purpose.

Knowing the *shōkaijō* system exists and knowing how to use it leads many individuals to specialize in taking advantage of it. Some people make a business of "selling" their status by giving introductions to persons and accepting valuable gifts and other favors in return. Advertising space salesmen in particular are notorious for taking advantage of the power of the *shōkaijō*.

These salesmen somehow get close to a businessman or well-known, respected and influential figure—the higher and more important the better—and get him to write a few words of introduction on several of his name cards. The introduction usually consists of only a few words, like "This is So & So. Please do what you can for him."

The salesmen then take these cards to the businessman's circle of friends in other companies and get advertising from them. There is little or no talk of advertising, and sometimes no "pitch" of any kind. The salesmen may only say that their publication would like to have the "support" of the company.

By this time, the man on the other end of the introduction knows exactly what is going on and more often than not, will hand over the amount of money suggested by the salesman, or approve the insertion of an advertisement to be billed later, without further conversation. Most companies in Japan have a special fund set aside, called *tsukiai-ryō*, "social debt funds," to pay off such "debts."

It should be emphasized, however, that the businessman who is put into a position in which he has to pay out *tsukiai-ryō* under such circumstances is fully aware that he is being "taken," and resents it strongly.

Hoshō-Nin
The Guarantor

The use of the *shōkaijō*, a deep-rooted social and business custom in Japan, derives its power from the practical and psychological need of the Japanese to have some kind of "guarantee" before they can bring themselves to become involved with someone with whom they do not have an *amae* relationship. Besides the *shōkaijō* itself, this need for a guarantor led to the development of another institutionalized function and figure in Japanese society, namely the *hoshōnin* or "guarantor."

In numerous cases involving official documents, establishing credit, and so on, the Japanese system requires a *hoshōnin* who accepts responsibility for the individual's character, trustworthiness and behavior. On a higher level, the person who gives a *shōkaijō* becomes partly and sometimes wholly responsible for whatever may come of it—both the good and the bad. A *hoshōnin*, by comparison, accepts full responsibility both in principle and in fact.

There are many cases when an introduction from one Japanese to another apparently has no more significance than the somewhat casual letter or note introductions common in the West, where nothing more complicated or compelling than simply courtesy is involved. But favors that are small and completely insignificant from the Western viewpoint are not bestowed lightly in Japan, especially when they occur through an introduction.

Chukai-Sha
The In-Between Man

The ultimate in the *shōkaijō* concept in Japan is the *chukai-sha* (chew-kie shah), or a person who acts as a go-between in business affairs. Of course the concept and role of the go-between is familiar in the West, but again, the Japanese have institutionalized the function. The *chukai-sha* in business and the *nakodo* (nah-coe-doe) in arranged marriages play a much greater and more important role in life in Japan.

The advantages of using a *chukai-sha* in business are numerous and not really mysterious. In the first place, the better go-betweens know just about everybody worth knowing—or know somebody else who knows them—and are respected and trusted individuals. In Japan where face-to-face communication by strangers is very difficult, the go-between can carry on most of the dialogue, help each side avoid losing face, and eventually smooth the way for the development of a formal relationship between the two parties if their interests merge.

The *chukai-sha* can be especially helpful to the foreign businessman in Japan, providing invaluable counsel on what to do and what not to do to maintain peace and harmony and negotiate successfully with Japanese companies. Recognizing this, some foreign companies operating in Japan have had *chukai-sha* on retainer for years.

O'Miyage
Giving to the Cause

Another important aspect of maintaining good relations, keeping *wa*, and getting things done in Japan comes under the general heading of gift-giving. There are, broadly speaking, three categories of gift-giving in Japan. On the lowest order are the *te-miyage* (tay-me-yah-gay) or "hand gifts" given to your host when you are invited to a Japanese home. *Te-miyage* usually consist of cake, pastries, boxes of fruit or perhaps traditional Japanese food delicacies. (It is not custom for the host to open these gifts while the guest is present.)

The second category of gifts are those given at year's end (New Year's) and in mid-summer on the occasion of *Obon* (Oh-bone), the Festival of the Dead. The end of the year is the most important of these two occasions, because this is when commercial firms are directly involved.

Companies are the biggest gift-givers in Japan. They give year-end gifts to "reward" customers for past patronage, to express gratitude, and to build up obligation for future business, etc. During the years that I had monthly printing done by *Dai Nippon* (Die Neep-pone), Japan's largest printing combine, the department in charge of my account had a case of beer or some other useful commodity delivered to my home every year just before New Year's. Being one of the largest printing companies in the world, with thousands of customers, one can imagine the size of Dai Nippon's annual year-end gift bill.

On an individual basis, subordinates give gifts to superiors, and people in general present gifts to *onjin* (own-gene)—benefactors to whom they are deeply obligated for past favors.

Most Japanese businessmen who go abroad take gifts of varying value to give to people they meet. For casual gifts to people who show them some hospitality, the visitors usually give relatively inexpensive gifts that are representative of Japan, such as folding fans, carved *kokeshi* (coe-kay-she) dolls, and the like. For important, established or potential business associates, the gifts are often quite expensive, or have considerable value for some other reason.

Because such gift-giving is institutionalized, the Japanese are naturally pleased when their foreign guests or business counterparts follow the custom. A set of golf clubs or a case of good Scotch is probably more appreciated in Japan than in any other country.

The third category of gift-giving in Japan comes under the heading of *O'tsukaimono* (Oh-t'sue-kie-mow-no)—"something to be used"—and is practiced at all times on every social and economic level. An *O'tsukaimono* gift is specifically given to a person when you are seeking a favor from that person. Rather than regard such gift-giving as a form of bribery, the Japanese feel that it is rude to ask a favor of someone without giving them something in return.

Gift-giving on an elaborate scale is not a recent development in Japan. Like so many other things, it has its roots deep in the culture, and in earlier times was as meticulously hedged in by rules as other areas of Japanese life. There were, in fact, specific rules prescribing exactly what item or thing was appropriate to give to people on particular occasions and according to their social rank. It was also prescribed as to how such gifts should be wrapped, using what materials in what manner. And finally, the procedure for presenting gifts to important superior-ranking persons was minutely detailed.

The importance attached to the proper choice, wrapping and presentation of gifts is apparent from the fact that well-to-do families often had one member whose primary responsibility was to know and advise the household on gift-giving protocol.

Mōshiwake Arimasen
Apology Without End

With so many areas of life so meticulously prescribed, it was virtually impossible for the Japanese of Feudal Japan to avoid all transgressions against their highly refined and aggressively enforced etiquette system. To compensate for the bonds their manners imposed upon them, and to help prevent the system from breaking down from its own weight, the Japanese gave great power to the apology. Most minor and many major transgressions against the system could be wiped clean by admission of guilt, an apology, and a demonstration of humility and regret.

An apologetic, humble attitude, especially by public figures, is still considered an essential virtue by the Japanese. In fact, for the Japanese to function smoothly within the web of their social obligations, it is necessary that they learn very early how and when to humiliate themselves—to apologize humbly. There are so many ways in which the Japanese can give or take offense, that the apology is also an institutionalized practice. The Japanese apologize for real as well as "pretended" shortcomings as often as Americans brag about their imagined ability and learning. The purpose of the Japanese apology is to avoid ill-will, friction, or anything else that might rub supersensitive people the wrong way.

The apology expressed by the term *sumimasen* (sue-me-mah-sin)—(literally, "it—the guilt I feel—is without end")—is the most common word for saying "I'm sorry" for small mistakes. *Mōshiwake-arimasen* (Moe-she-wah-kay ah-ree-mah-sin)—"I have no excuse" (and submit myself to your mercy), is used in more serious situations. These terms, expressed several times amidst much bowing and facial signs of humility and sorrow, are often followed by *O'yurushi kudasai* (Oh-you-rue-she koo-dah-sie)—"Please forgive me."

Within the context of the Japanese system, the greatest sin is to be guilty of a crime, of any kind, and refuse to admit or express regret over it. Thus exceptional importance is attached to the apology.

For a Japanese (also Koreans and Chinese) to confess to a transgression, apologize and express sincere regret, is more or less the same in the Western sense as a guilty person being punished and rehabilitated at the same time. If the admission and apology are sincere, the Japanese forgive completely (rather than demand long-term punishment as is the case in the West).

Ojigi
Politeness Makes Perfect

The first-time visitor to Japan is always struck by the wonderful politeness of the people. No other Japanese trait or accomplishment has come in for so much praise. But there is an element of misunderstanding inherent in accepting this politeness at face value, because it often misleads Westerners who are unfamiliar with the character and role of traditional Japanese etiquette.

For one thing, not all of the famous politeness of the Japanese should be automatically equated with feelings of kindness, regard or respect for others—a reaction that is all too common where first-time visitors to Japan are concerned.

The Japanese are, of course, perfectly capable of being polite in the fullest sense of the word and probably are genuinely more polite than most other people, but what the foreigner sees, and is often overly impressed by, is strictly a mechanical role that has little or nothing to do with the personal feelings of the individuals concerned.

Many Westerners, especially Americans of the tourist variety, lavish praise upon the Japanese for this formal politeness. But most are basing their judgment of Japanese politeness on such things as the pretty doll-like elevator and escalator girls who work in department stores and deluxe hotels. These girls, picked for looks and dressed in cute uniforms, stand and bow and repeat the same lines all day long in self-effacing, heart-rendering voices that remind one of the chirping of baby birds that have fallen out of their nest.

The *Ojigi* (oh-jee-gee) or "bow" is the most visible manifestation of Japan's traditional etiquette. It is used for both greetings and farewells, when expressing appreciation or thanks, when apologizing, when asking for an important favor—and when requesting *any* kind of action from a government bureaucrat.

The occasion and the parties involved in an *Ojigi* determine the kind of bow that is appropriate. The lower the bow and the longer one holds the position, the stronger the indication of respect, gratitude, sincerity, obeisance, humility, contriteness, etc.

Generally speaking, there are three kinds or degrees of bowing: the "informal" bow, the "formal" bow and the "deep" bow—*saikeirei* (sie-kay-ee-raye), which means "highest form of salutation." In the light, informal bow, the body is bent at approximately a 15-degree angle with the hands at the sides. This bow is used for all casual occasions between people of all rank.

The formal bow requires that the body be bent to about 30-degrees, with the hands together, palms down, on the knees. Ordinarily the bower holds this pose for only two or three seconds, then automatically returns to the upright position. If the other party remains bowed for a longer period, it is polite for the recipient to bow again. The other party may bow a second and third time. Synchronizing the bows so that both parties rise at approximately the same time can be tricky, and sometimes unintentionally embarrassing.

When one party wants to emphasize the salutation and holds the pose for an unusually long period of time—while intoning appropriate remarks—the recipient must continue to make short bows, usually of a gradually lessening degree, to properly acknowledge the other bower's action.

The slow, deep *saikeirei* bow, which was the bow used to Emperors in earlier days, is only occasionally used now, generally by elderly people—who have a tendency to go back to the old ways as they grow older.

Businessmen who go to *ryōkan* (rio-khan) inns or *geisha* houses may be greeted by maids or *geisha* who bow to them while sitting on the floor. It is not necessary to get down on the floor to return the bow—but it can be the beginning of a lot of fun!

The Japanese reputation for politeness breaks down very easily and quickly in many situations, particularly in those involving government offices, and often in business contexts as well. I have often gone into business offices in which there were dozens of people and had to go to extreme lengths to get someone to acknowledge my presence. At first, I thought this peculiar reaction was brought on by the fact that I was a foreigner. Since the Japanese usually never expect a foreigner to be able to speak their language, I was prepared to believe they hesitated to say anything because no one could speak English; or were simply bashful. It soon became obvious, however, that Japanese visitors were also frequently subjected to the same treatment, particularly in government offices.

Further observation and experience taught me how to shorten the period of waiting—at least in business offices—but direct action on my part was still required. This consisted of catching the eye of anyone in the office who glanced up at me, then bowing very rapidly before he or she could turn away. The most effective bow to use in this situation, it seems, is a short, jerky one. This action triggers an automatic reflex in the Japanese and the party bows back, thus acknowledging your presence. He or she is then strongly obligated to follow up this step by coming to you or sending someone to you to find out what you want.

Another element in Japanese politeness (outside of unexpected visits to business offices) is the compulsion so many Japanese feel to go out of their way to make sure every foreign visitor, whether businessman or tourist, has a good time and leaves with a good impression of the country and its people. As a result of this syndrome, the Japanese are famous for their hospitality, and visitors who are not used to this kind of treatment are often overwhelmed by it.

The main point for the foreign businessman to keep in mind is that he should not confuse the politeness or the hospitality of the Japanese with either weakness on their part or strength on his part. If he is really being courted by the Japanese, he may in fact have to eventually limit the amount of hospitality he accepts, to avoid being put at a serious disadvantage, physically as well as psychologically. Most Japanese businessmen are conditioned to regular drinking bouts. They also regularly bargain as a group. The lone visitor who goes into a bargaining session with a Japanese team after several nights on the town has his work cut out for him.

Kyōsō
Competition by the Numbers

Before the advent of the modern era in Japan, most personal competition, especially within groups, was taboo because it results in friction and disharmony—the opposite of *wa*. The Japanese, were in fact, taught that competition for personal, selfish purposes was criminal.

While there are now many areas and ways in which the Japanese compete against each other fiercely, especially in education, the Japanese business system in general has maintained all the old sanctions against individual competition, and continues to promote the concept and practice of group action and team spirit.

There are other cultural factors involved in the taboos against personal competition among the Japanese. One of the worst things that can befall any Japanese is to be shamed and made to lose "face." Personal competition, with a few sanctioned exceptions such as in athletic contests, always carries with it the danger of being shamed.

The important thing for the foreign businessman to remember is that his contacts in Japanese companies, regardless of their rank, are not "officially" in competition with their own colleagues, and will resist any attitude or behavior that might make them appear to be competing against their own co-workers.

There have been and still are numerous occasions when the foreign businessman says in effect to a Japanese contact, "Look! You cooperate with me and help me get this deal through, and it will make you a big man in your company!" The one thing that would inevitably make it impossible for a Japanese to reach the higher or highest echelons of his company would be to break step with his co-workers; to strike out on his own.

Even though the Japanese are imbued with a compulsion to better themselves, to rise to the same level as those who are higher, and even though this compulsion is one of the prime forces motivating the Japanese economy, the extraordinary drive this gives the Japanese must generally be channeled into group-effort within the framework of the Japanese company system.

Jichō
Staying Out of Trouble

Another distinctive feature of Japanese life that is designed to promote *wa*, and help the individual maintain essential dignity, is expressed in the word *jichō* (jee-choe), which means "to respect one's self"; to be prudent.

As is so often the case, however, respecting one's self in the Japanese context is not exactly the same as within Western cultures. Practicing *jichō* means to do nothing that would result in criticism, thereby lessening one's chances for success. It means to be exquisitely wary of getting involved in anything that might make one stand out from the crowd and become subject to criticism.

Chapter 4

Kaisha
The Japanese Company

Uchi-No Kaisha
Companies as "Family-Clans"

In Japanese, the word for company, *kaisha* (kie-shah), has strong connotations of "community." In referring to their place of employment, the Japanese typically use the term *uchi* (ou-chee), which means "inside" or "my house," in a possessive sense—*uchi-no kaisha* or "my company." This means a lot more than "the place where I work."

For those Japanese who work for larger, well-known companies, the place where they work, *shokuba* (show-coo-bah), takes precedence over the profession or kind of work they do. When asked what they do for a living, the Japanese generally will not say they are teachers, engineers, carpenters, salesmen or whatever. They will say they are members of the staff of Chiyoda High School, of Sanyo Electric Company, of Takenaka Construction Company or Nissan Motors. Profession, *shokugyō* (show-coo-ghee-yoe) takes a back seat to *shokuba* (place of work).

The degree to which the Japanese identify with their employers is generally so strong it prevents them from having or developing any interest or links with others in their profession. In many professions, members of different organizations do, in fact, avoid communicating with each other.

In the U.S., two people in any work category can often establish a deep and satisfying rapport within minutes of their first meeting, even under the most casual or incidental circumstances. Such relationships can be especially deep and satisfying if the two happen to be in the same profession, whether they are truck drivers, bakers or doctors. In Japan, such spontaneous horizontal relationships are practically out of the question.

The fact that the loyalty of the individual Japanese worker or manager is almost totally absorbed by his own seniority-ranked group makes it difficult for him to establish close relationships with any outsider, including those who are in the same line of work. On the contrary, there is a special feeling of wariness and sometimes hostility between Japanese and their professional counterparts within as well as outside their own companies.

The exclusivity inherent in the vertically ranked company system in Japan is so powerful that it makes it difficult, and sometimes impossible, for a group or a company to do business with another group or firm with which it does not have "established relations." When a company for some unavoidable reason is forced to engage in a business transaction with someone or some organization without close, personal ties having already been established, they refer to it as "doing business with the enemy."

This taboo is so deeply engrained it sometimes leads to absolutely ludicrous situations—such as a company failing to act on a vital piece of information simply because it did not come from someone with whom they have "personal relations."

Another of the things that seems especially strange to the foreign businessman is the fact that in Japan it is not always the most capable or hardest working man who is most likely to be promoted. The seniority system notwithstanding, the rank-and-file Japanese do not like for the professionally superior man to be promoted. They are afraid he will end up being more concerned about himself than his fellow workers. The Japanese way is to promote the man who gets along with everybody, is good at maintaining harmony, is flexible, and can be expected to be concerned with the welfare of all.

Recognition and advancement in Japanese companies does not depend so much on ability or achievement as upon length of service with the company, age, amount of schooling, which school the employee attended, and having the right attitude. The young man who wants to go up the executive escalator smoothly tends to do so by quietly building up seniority and practicing *jichō*—"respecting himself." This means, again, that he will take every precaution not to invite criticism or attract undue attention to himself; never be forward; never question his superiors; that he will more or less merge himself with the furniture and wait his turn.

No doubt the key reason why the superior/subordinate ranking system in Japanese society is so powerful is because it makes everyone totally dependent on those above and below them. Each member must do his or her own part to avoid jeopardizing the entire group. With this in mind, it is not difficult to understand why a 30-year old assistant section chief in Mitsui & Company or Hitachi or Suzuki Electric is not about to disturb the harmony he has with his co-workers, inferiors or superiors, since he is likely to spend his whole working life with them, and his contentment and success depend upon their continuing good will.

Shikomu
Training in "Company Morality"

The Japanese like to say "The enterprise is the people," meaning that a company cannot be separated from the people who make it up; that members of a company are bound together by emotional, economic and social ties transcending all others. The Japanese do not believe an employee can or will make his full contribution to the enterprise unless he is totally committed to the company, and gives it his highest loyalty. This is another one of the reasons why major Japanese firms prefer to hire employees directly from school, when they are young and "unspoiled" and more susceptible to being imbued with the company philosophy.

The training Japanese companies put new employees through to instill their particular philosophy is referred to as *shikomu* (she-coe-moo), which is a special kind of training that includes not only techniques, but the morality and philosophy of the action. The master carpenter in Old Japan, for example, used to send his apprentice to the theater to learn the ethics of life. When the apprentice later made a mistake with the hammer or saw, the master would upbraid him and asked if he had not yet learned anything at the theater.

The Japanese philosophy is that the company with good human relations will succeed, while the company with bad human relations will fail. The smooth functioning of human relations within companies, at least in principle, takes precedence over what the section, department and sometimes even the company is supposed to accomplish.

This human-relations type of management preferred by the Japanese is based on face-to-face physical contact within groups, and with individuals in other groups with whom they have established relations. This, of course, is another aspect of the role of introductions and go-betweens, and explains why the Japanese business system precludes, or makes difficult, conducting business by phone until face-to-face contact has been made, and a basis for a substantial degree of *amae* established.

Shakai No Kurabu
The Company as a Social Club

Akio Morita, one of the founders of the fabulously successful Sony Corporation, once remarked that Japanese companies "look" more like social organizations than business enterprises. Morita was, of course, referring not only to the junior/senior, parent/child vertical structure of Japanese companies, but also to the famous "paternalism" of the larger ones.

To understand and work with a Japanese company, it is indeed helpful to think of it in terms of a cross between an exclusive club, a cooperative union and, lastly, a business enterprise—because it incorporates attributes of all three of these.

Japanese industry as a whole is characterized by the existence of a few huge companies that dominate each particular industrial category and are usually aligned with a Zaibatsu-like group of other firms. Beneath these giant companies is a thicker layer of medium-sized firms, some of them independent and others satellite to one of the larger enterprises. Way below these two upper layers is a mass of small to miniscule shop-factories that are mostly dependent on the larger firms for their day-to-day existence.

Ichiryū, Niryū, Sanryū
First-Class, Second-Class, Third-Class

All of Japan's enterprises across the board are first classified according to industrial category, then by size and market share, and finally by whatever group of companies the individual firm may be affiliated with. All of the larger and more important firms in each industrial category are ranked by their fellow members, as well as others, in relation to their standing when compared to all other enterprises in the same category. A top-ranked company is called an *ichi-ryū* (ee-chee-ree-you) or "first-class" company. A *ni-ryū* (nee-ree-you) is a "second-class" company; a *san-ryū* (sahn-ree-you) is a "third-class" company. Those below third-class are seldom ranked.

The gap between *ichi-ryū* companies and most *ni-ryū* firms is usually considerable, emphasizing the fact that each industrial category in the country tends to be made up of a few very large firms and a large number of medium and small firms. The ranking of the firms in the second and third classes is not always as clearcut as among the *ichi-ryū*, but the leading *ni-ryū* and *san-ryū* firms are very conscious of their relative ranking, and continuously strive to elevate themselves to a higher class.

Competition for the title and prestige of *ichi-ryū* company is also intense—and continuous—often going beyond what Western businessmen regard as rational behavior. This is part of the motivation that spurs the Japanese economy.

Just as Japanese companies continuously vie to achieve or maintain the highest rank, competition among young Japanese high school and college graduates to enter *ichi-ryū* companies is equally intense. Until recent years at least, working for a first-class company was more important to most Japanese than pure economic considerations, because social status was primarily determined by place of employment. Traditionally in Japan, social status took precedence over economic status, and still today the social motive often out-ranks the profit motive (a value many non-Japanese find hard to swallow).

The prestige of working for a first-ranked company in Japan extends from the chief executive officers down to the lowest laborer, and in fact constitutes a kind of economic caste system.

Another characteristic of Japanese industry is for each of the larger firms to "attach" to themselves a host of smaller, subsidiary or affiliated firms known as *ko-gaisha* (coe-guy-shah), or "child-companies"—which are also ranked.

These *ko-gaisha* are generally divided into two categories: *chokkei kigyo* (choke-kay-ee keeg-yoe) or "direct-line" companies; and *keiretsu kaisha* (kay-ee-rate-sue kie-shah) or "aligned companies." Direct-line companies in this terminology and practice resemble wholly owned subsidiaries. The relationship between "aligned" companies and the larger "parent" companies is less precise and less intimate. The parent company may supply capital to the aligned child company and provide various marketing functions. The "degree" of the alignment, ultimately, is determined by the percentage of its production it is obligated to sell to the parent company, which in turn determines its dependence on the larger firm.

Jūyaku
"Big" Executives

As in most enterprises everywhere, there are three categories of personnel in a larger Japanese company, the *Jimukei* (Jee-moo-kay-ee) or administrative personnel; the *Gijutsu-kei* (ghee-joot-sue-kay-ee) or technical personnel; and the *Ippan* (Eep-pahn) or "common" staff. This is one of the few similarities between Japanese and non-Japanese firms. For one thing, larger Japanese companies hire *only* college graduates for administrative positions. Examples of junior and senior high school graduates making their way up the managerial hierarchy in Japanese companies are rare indeed.

There are also three levels of employees in larger Japanese companies. These are the *yaku-in* (yah-coo-eene) or executives from director on up; the *bukachō* (boo-cah-choe), or middle-lower management made up of department and section heads and their assistants; and the *hira-shain* (he-rah shah-eene), or employees without rank. The following table gives the administrative titles (grades) commonly found in Japanese companies:

Kabunushi (Cah-boo-new-she)..................... Stockholders

Torishimariyakukai........................... Board of Directors
  (Toe-ree-she-mah-ree-yah-coo-kie)

Kaichō (Kie-choe)....................... Chairman of the Board

Daihyō Torishimariyaku .... Representative Director
  (Die-he-yoe Toe-ree-she-mah-ree-yah-coo)

Shachō (Shah-choe)............................... President

Senmu Torishimariyaku .... Director & Executive Vice President
  (Same-moo Toe-ree-she-mah-ree-yah-coo)

Jōmu Torishimariyaku .... Director & Senior Vice President
(Joe-moo Toe-ree-she-mah-ree-yah-coo)

Jōnin Kansayaku .... Standing Auditor
(Joe-neen Khan-sah-yah-coo)

*Buchō (Boo-choe) .... Department Head

Kachō (Cah-choe) .... Section Head

Kakarichō (Cah-cah-ree-choe) .... Supervisor

Hira-shain (He-rah-shah-eene) .... Unranked employees

Each Japanese company usually has one or more *daihyotorishimariyaku*—a director who has power of attorney to act in the name of the company. Besides the regular *buchō* (department chiefs), companies may also have *Semmon-buchō* (Same-moan boo-choe), "Specialty" *buchō*, or individuals who have been promoted to the rank of *buchō* because of their professional skill or knowledge, but have no department under them.

Hako-No Naka Ni Hitobito
People in Boxes

The basic organizational and operating unit in most larger Japanese companies is a section or sub-section, made up of a few to several persons. Each section *(ka)* consists of a section chief *(kachō)*, usually two assistants or supervisors *(kakarichō)*, and several staff members. Several sections combined make up a department *(bu)*, headed by a department chief *(buchō)*.

The physical make-up in a section is a "box"—desks arranged to form a rectangular box-shape, with the manager and his assistants at the front or head of the formation, and the junior members strung out along the sides. Each department is made up of several of these "boxes."

The desk of the department chief is usually farthest from the door, near a window if there is one, commanding a good view of the entire department. Generally, the only

---

*In large companies, some *bucho* may also be corporate directors.

managers in a Japanese company who have private offices are executive directors and up, in larger companies.

Within each of these basic boxes, responsibility and activity is more or less a team thing, with work assigned to the group as a whole. Members of each section are expected to cooperate and support each other. Older, more experienced members provide new members with the direction and help they need, in a continuous on-the-job training process. The effectiveness of a particular section is strongly influenced by the total morale, ambition and talent of the whole team.

Just as individuals within the section "boxes" are ranked according to their seniority and title (and unofficially according to their overall attitude and effectiveness), the "boxes" are also ranked according to their importance within the departments they make up. The larger the number of people in a box, the more important that section is likely to be. The more sections in a department, the more important that department.

Managers are very much aware of the rank of their sections and departments, and are naturally concerned about being assigned to a "box" or department ranked below what they "know" their own seniority and experience deserves.

This organizational structure within a Japanese company is rigid, and therefore does not contribute to specialization, speedy results or innovations. To counter this handicap, Japanese companies also make use of special project teams to cope with and take advantage of new technological and management developments—leading some of the critics of the present system to predict that these teams will eventually replace the "box-sections" altogether.

Bu
Finding the Right One

Most of the departments in Japanese companies are similar in name to comparable departments in Western companies. In function, however, there are some outstanding exceptions. Namely, the General Affairs Department, *Sōmu Bu* (So-moo Boo), and the Personnel Department, *Jinji Bu* (Gene-jee Boo).

The *Sōmu Bu* has no exact counterpart in Western firms, but is a key department in most larger Japanese enterprises. It does such things as provide liaison with customers, coordinate inter-departmental relations and handle company mail, and is in charge of telephone switchboards, maintenance, official files, stock ledgers, etc. It is the *Sōmu Bu* that provides the receptionists who greet callers, so most initial contacts with Japanese companies are with this department.

The *Jinji Bu* or Personnel Department in a Japanese company is generally larger and much more powerful than its counterpart in a Western company. It makes practically all of the decisions as to who is hired, where they are initially assigned, and when and where they are rotated as part of their continuous on-the-job training.

Among other typical departments in larger Japanese companies: *Kokusai Bu* (Coke-sie Boo), the International Department; *Seizō Bu* (Say-ee-zoe Boo), Production Department; *Kikaku Bu* (Key-cah-coo Boo), Planning Department; *Shizai Bu* (She-zie Boo), Purchasing Department; *Shogai Bu* (Show-guy Boo), Public Relations Department; *Keiri Bu* (Kay-ee-ree Boo), Accounting Department; *Eigyō Bu* (Aa-e-ghee-yoe Boo), Sales Department; *Kohō Bu* (Coe-hoe Boo), Advertising Department.

While the names of these departments are familiar, they, like the management categories, have their own unique Japanese character.

In addition to the various *bu* (departments), some large Japanese companies also have what is called the *Shachoshitsu* (Shah-choe-sheet-sue), or "President's Office." This is a team that performs staff work for the president of the company. The functions of the *Shachoshitsu* vary in different firms, and may include secretarial work, record-keeping, planning and management information systems.

The grouping or sectionalization by and within Japanese organizations has a number of serious drawbacks in business. It hinders and in many instances completely blocks communication, not only within the individual group itself but also between groups, including those within the same organization or enterprise. The reason for this is that in an exclusive, tightly knit, vertically aligned group, communication is more or less limited to moving upward or downward, and in most cases must go through every senior member in each level of the hierarchy. If one member is absent or chooses not to act, the communication may be short-circuited. This vertical structure also makes horizontal communication with "outsiders" difficult because individual links in the structure are generally not authorized to make decisions or engage in business negotiations on their own.

Even the top man generally cannot act as spokesman for the group without first reaching a consensus of opinion among his co-workers and fellow managers, regardless of the subject matter. This process of consensus naturally takes time, and also incorporates the possibility that there may be no response, since it is more difficult to get five or seven or more people to agree on anything. This also is one of the primary reasons why it is usually difficult for an outsider (a journalist, for example) to call up a Japanese company and get any kind of official policy statement—or sometimes just a simple detail about the company's activities.

Another disadvantage of the *sempai-kōhai* grouping system is that its exclusivity contributes to the non-cooperative spirit and even hostility with which the Japanese view outsiders. Since they are bound to the group, members do not want anyone upsetting its balance or harmony in any way. There is thus very little and sometimes no communication between departments in some companies, with the result that the manager of one department may know little or nothing about what is going on in other departments. This sectionalism is so intense in some organizations that a kind of internal warfare rages. Rivalry between sections and departments in service-type companies such as public relations and advertising is often especially fierce, making it even more difficult for the client or customer who must deal with more than one group in the company.

Further, a management system based on personal loyalty within a group, and on seniority, makes it very difficult for Japanese managers to shift from job-to-job or company-to-company, even when they have the still rare opportunity to do so. The emotions aroused when this system is ignored or breaks down—as happened in many joint-venture operations established in the 1950s and 60s—invariably leads to unsatisfactory if not disasterous results. Being very much aware of these dangers, really top-flight Japanese managers generally try to shun joint-ventures, leaving them to "second-string" personnel, or those near or already in forced retirement.

The problems involved in forming a new company with "old" employees in Japan are formidable. The Japanese often accept the premise that the managers first assigned to such an undertaking are little more than caretakers. They take a long-range view, resigning themselves to waiting for several years for capable people to come up from the bottom in the new company.

Despite its various failings, however, the grouping factor in Japanese business management results in motivation that is both powerful and dynamic. Like the villagers of Feudal Japan who could increase their social status only by out-producing their neighbors, members of the individual groups in Japanese companies can enhance their own prestige only by increasing the effectiveness and importance of their group. This instills in each member a powerful urge not only to protect the rights and interests of the group, but to also make it stand out from competing sections.

Bōnenkai
Meeting to Forget

Japan's personally oriented management system, with its strict rules requiring workers to repress their individualism in the interest of group harmony, naturally results in friction and the build-up of stress. There are two popular annual activities partly aimed at helping to relieve these personal antagonisms: the *Bōnenkai* (Bow-nane-kie), "Forget the Old Year Party," and *Shinnenkai* (Sheen-nane-kie), "New Year Party."

The theme of the traditional end-of-the-year *Bōnenkai* meeting, held at the place of work and marked by food and drinks being ordered in, is to have a good time with co-workers and forgive and forget all the bad things that happened during the course of the year. There is no set date for the *Bōnnenkai*. Some companies hold them several days before the last working day of the year.

New Year's, *O'Shogatsu* (Oh-Show-gah-t'sue), is Japan's major holiday. Almost everyone is off from work for three or four days, and some companies close for a longer period. The occasion is used for family and shrine visits. In most offices and companies, the first day after the New Year's break there is an informal "Open-house" type *Shinnenkai* meeting. The purpose of the meeting is to formally greet co-workers and superiors and ask all of them to once again "indulge" you for another year. It is also felt that beginning the new year on a happy, positive note will have a beneficial effect on morale and productivity the rest of the year. Usually, little or no work is done on this day. Women employees, particularly younger ones, often wear their prettiest kimonos on this occasion.

It is also customary at this time of year for company representatives to visit their banks,* and for suppliers to visit companies that buy from them. The callers first greet their contacts with, *Akemashite shinnen O'medetō gozaimasu* (Ah-kay-mahsh-tay sheen-nane Oh-may-day-toe-go-zie-mah-sue)—Congratulations on the opening of the New Year, or "Happy New Year!"

---

*Japanese businessmen are generally much more deeply obligated to their banks than their foreign counterparts. Many banks own substantial equity in anywhere from a few to dozens of companies.

This is immediately followed by the set expression: *Sakunen-chu wa taihen Osewa-ni narimashita. Mata konnen-mo yoroshiku Onegai itashimasu* (Sah-coo-nane-chew wah tie-hane Oh-say-wah-nee nah-ree-mah-she-tah. Mah-tah kone-nane moe yoe-roe-she-coo Oh-nay-guy-ee-tah-she-mah-sue).

This means, loosely: "We are deeply obligated to you for your patronage last year, and offer you our deepest gratitude. We ask you to please continue doing business with us this year."

Chapter 5

Manejimento
Aspects of Japanese Company Management

Shūshinkōyō
It's For Life

Probably the most talked about and notorious facet of Japan's family-patterned company system is *shūshinkōyō* (shu-sheen-coe-yoe), or "life-time employment"—which applies, however, to only an elite minority of the nation's workers. Although a direct descendant of Feudal Japan, when peasants and craftsmen were attached to a particular clan by birth, the life-time employment system did not become characteristic of large-scale modern Japanese industry until the 1950s. In the immediate postwar period, losing one's job was tantamount to being sentenced to starvation. To prevent employees from being fired or arbitrarily laid off, national federation union leaders took advantage of their new freedom and the still weak position of industry to force adoption of the *shūshinkōyō* system by the country's major enterprises.

Under the life-time employment system, all *permanent* employees of larger companies and government bureaus are, in practice, hired for life. These organizations generally hire only once a year, directly from schools. Some time before the end of the school year, each company and government ministry or office decides on how many new people it wants to bring in. The company or government bureau then invites students who are to graduate that year (in some cases only from certain universities) to take competitive written and oral company examinations for employment.

One company, for example, may plan on taking 200 university graduates as administrative trainees, and 500 junior and senior high school graduates for placement in blue-collar work. Since "permanent" employment is "for life," companies are careful to select candidates who have well-rounded personalities, and are judged most likely to adjust to that particular company's "style."

This method of employee selection is known as *shikakuseido* (she-cah-coo-say-ee-doe) or "personal qualification system." This means that new employees are selected on the basis of their education, character, personality, and family backgrounds; as opposed to work experience or technological backgrounds.

A larger company hiring new employees, and firms entering into new business tie-ups in Japan, are sometimes compared to arranged (Japanese-style) marriages, and the analogy is a good one. Both employment and joint-venture affiliations are, in principle, for life. Both parties therefore want to be sure not only of the short-term intentions of the potential partner, but also of their character and personality —even if there are any "black sheep" in the family. Thus both prospective employee and potential business partner must undergo close scrutiny. When the Japanese commit themselves, the commitment is expected to be total.

Choosing employees on the basis of personal qualifications is especially important to Japanese managers and supervisors on a personal level. Generally speaking, they themselves cannot hire, fire, or hold back promotions. They must manage by "tact," by getting and keeping the trust, goodwill and cooperation of their subordinates.

Besides exercising control over employee candidates by allowing only students from certain universities to take their entrance examinations, many companies also depend upon well-known professors in specific universities to recommend choice candidates to them each year. The reputations of some professors, especially in the physical sciences, is often such that they can actually "parcel out" their best students from each of their graduating classes to top firms in the field.

Nenkō Jōretsu
The "Merit of Years"

Once hired by a larger company, the permanent Japanese employee who is a university graduate is on the first rung of a pay/promotion escalator system that over the years will gradually, and automatically, take him to or near the upper management level. This is the famous (or infamous) *Nenkō Jōretsu* (Nane-coe Joe-ray-t'sue) "long service rank" or seniority system, under which pay and promotions are based on longevity first, and ability and accomplishment second.

Not surprisingly, the employee, at least in administrative areas, is considered more important than the job in the Japanese company system. As a result, job classifications on the administrative level may be fairly clear, but specific duties of individuals tend to be ill-defined or not defined at all. Work is more or less assigned on a collective basis, and each employee tends to work according to his or her ability and inclinations. Those who are capable, diligent and ambitious, naturally do most of the work. Those who turn out to be lazy or incompetent are given tasks befitting their ability and interests.

Young management-trainee employees are switched from one job to another every two or three years, and in larger companies are often transferred to other office or plant locations. Reason for this is to expose them to a wide range of experiences so they will be more valuable to the company as they advance up the promotional ladder. Individuals are "monitored" and informally rated, and eventually the more capable are promoted faster than the other members of their age group. The ones promoted the fastest usually become managing directors; and one of their number becomes president.

Instead of faster promotions and more pay raises during the first 12 to 15 years, the most capable and productive people get status. If they prove to be equally capable in their personal relations with others, they are the ones who are eventually singled out to reach the upper levels of the managerial hierarchy.

The seniority system in Japanese companies takes ordinary, even incapable people who have toed the company line and made no blunders, to the head of departments, and occasionally to the head of companies. But their limitations are recognized, and the department or company is run by competent people below them, with little or no damage to the egos of the less capable executives or to the overall harmony within the firm.

Each work-section in a Japanese company is three-layered, consisting of young on-the job trainees (a status that often lasts for several years); mature, experienced workers who carry most of the burden; and older employees whose productivity has fallen off due to their age.

Direct, specific orders do not set well with the members of these work-sections. This leaves them with the impression they are not trusted, and that management has no "respect" for them. Even the lowest clerk or delivery boy in a company is very sensitive about being treated with respect. The Japanese say they prefer "ambiguous" general instructions. All the work groups want from management are "goals and direction."

Because human relations are given precedence in the Japanese management system, great importance is attached to the "unity of employees" within each of these groups. The primary responsibility of the senior manager in a group is not directing the people in their work, but making "adjustments" among them in order to maintain harmonious relations within the group.

"What is required of the ideal manager," say the Japanese, "is that he know how to adjust human relations rather than be knowledgeable about the operation of his department or the overall function of the company. In fact, the man who is competent and works hard is not likely to be popular with other members of his group, and as a result does not make a good manager," they add.

Besides being "somewhat incompetent" as far as work is concerned while being skilled at preventing inter-employee friction, the ideal Japanese manager has one other important trait. He is willing to shoulder all the responsibility for any mistakes or failings of his subordinates—hopefully, of course, without any loss of face.

The efficient operation of this "group system" is of course based on personal obligations and trust between the manager and his staff. The manager must make his staff obligated to him in order to keep their cooperation and in order to ensure that none of them will deliberately do anything or leave anything undone that would cause him embarrassment. Whatever knowledge and experience is required for the group to be productive is found among the manager's subordinates if he is weak in this area.

Seishin
Training in Spirit

The Japanese associate productivity with employees having *seishin* (say-e-sheen) or "spirit," and being imbued with "Japanese morality." Company training therefore covers not only technical areas, but also moral, philosophical, aesthetic and political factors. Each of the larger companies has its own particular "company philosophy" and image, which is incorporated into its training and indoctrination programs. This is one of the prime reasons why major Japanese companies prefer not to hire older, experienced "outsiders," it being assumed that they could not wholly accept or fit into the company mold.

Onjō Shugi
"Mothering" Employees

The amount of loyalty, devotion and hard work displayed by most Japanese employees is in direct proportion to the paternalism, *onjō shugi* (own-joe-shu-gee), of the company. The more paternalistic (maternalistic would seem to be the better word) the company, the harder working and the more devoted and loyal employees tend to be. Japanese style paternalism includes the concept that the employer is totally responsible for the livelihood and well-being of all employees, and must be willing to go all the way for an employee when the need arises.

The degree of paternalism in Japanese companies varies tremendously, with some of them literally practicing cradle-to-grave responsibility for employees and their families. Many managers thus spend a great deal of time participating in social events involving their staff members—child-births, weddings, funerals, and so on.

Fringe benefits make up a very important part of the income of most Japanese workers, and include such things as housing or housing subsidies, transportation allowances, family allowances, children allowances, health services, free recreational facilities, educational opportunities, retirement funds, etc.

The wide range of fringe benefits received by Japanese employees are an outgrowth of spiraling inflation and an increasingly heavy income tax system during the years between 1945 and 1955. Companies first began serving employees free lunches. Then larger companies built dormitories, apartments and houses. Eventually, recreational, educational and medical facilities were added to employee benefits.

Japan's famous twice-a-year bonuses, *Shōyo* (Show-yoe), were originally regarded as a fringe benefit by employees and management, but workers and unions have long since considered them an integral part of wages. Unions prefer to call the bonuses *Kimatsu Teate* (Key-maht'sue Tay-ah-tay), or Seasonal Allowances. The bonuses, usually the equivalent of two to six or eight months of base wages, are paid in mid-summer just before *Obon* (Oh-bone), a major Buddhist festival honoring the dead, and just before the end of the calendar year in December.

Rinjisaiyō
The Outsiders

Not all employees of Japanese companies, including the larger ones, are hired for life or come under the *nenkō jōretsu* system of pay and promotion. There are two distinct categories of employees in most Japanese companies:— those who are hired as permanent employees under the *shūshinkōyō* and *nenkō jōretsu* systems, and those hired as *rinjisaiyō* (reen-jee-sie-yoe) or "temporary appointment" workers. The latter may be hired by the day or by the year but they cannot be hired on a longer than a year contract. They are paid at a lower scale than permanent employees, and may be let go at any time.

The *rinjisaiyō* system of temporary employees is of course a direct outgrowth of the disadvantages of a permanent employment system, which at most is viable only in a booming, continuously growing economy.

Ringi Seido
Putting it in Writing

In addition to the cooperative-work approach based on each contributing according to his ability and desire, many larger Japanese companies divide and diversify management responsibility by a system known as *ringi seido* (reen-gee say-ee-doe), which means, more or less, "written proposal system." This is a process by which management decisions are based on proposals made by lower level managers, and is responsible for the "bottoms-up" management associated with many Japanese companies.

Briefly, the *ringi* system consists of proposals calling for management decisions, written by the initiating section or department, then circulated horizontally and vertically to all layers of management for approval. Managers and executives who approve of the proposal stamp the document with their name seals, *hanko* (hahn-coe), in the prescribed place. Anyone who disapproves, passes the document on without stamping it—or puts his seal on sideways or upside down to indicate conditional approval. When approval is not unanimous, higher executives may send the document back with recommendations that more staff work be done on it, or that the opinions of those who disapprove be taken into consideration. Managers may attach comments to the proposal if they wish.

In practice, the man who originates a *ringi-sho* (written proposal "document") informally consults with other managers before submitting it for official scrutiny. He may work for weeks or months in his efforts to get the idea approved unofficially. If he runs into resistance, he will invariably seek help from colleagues who owe him favors. They in turn will approach others who are obligated to them.

The efficiency and effectiveness of the *ringi seido* varies with the company. In some it is little more than a formality, and there is pressure from the top to eliminate the system altogether. In other companies the system reigns supreme, and there is strong opposition toward any talk of eliminating it. The system is so deeply entrenched in both the traditional management philosophy of the Japanese and in the aspirations and ambitions of younger managers that it will no doubt be around for a long time.

The foreign businessman negotiating with a Japanese company should be aware that his proposals may be the subject of one or more *ringi-sho* which not only takes up a great deal of time (they must be circulated in the proper chain-of-status order), it also exposes them to the scrutiny of as many as a dozen or more individuals whose interests and attitudes may differ.

Whether or not a *ringi* proposal is approved by the president is primarily determined by who has approved it by the time it gets to him. If all or most of the more important managers concerned have stamped the *ringi-sho*, chances are the president will also approve it.

While this system is cumbersome and slow, generally speaking it helps build and maintain a cooperative spirit within companies. In addition, it assures that when a policy change or new program is initiated, it will have the support of the majority of managers.

As can be seen from the still wide-spread use of the *ringi seido*, top managers in many Japanese companies are not always planners or decision-makers. Their main function is to see to it that the company operates smoothly and efficiently as a team, to see that new managers are nurtured within the system, and to "pass judgment" on decisions proposed by junior managers.

Nemawashi
Behind the Scenes

Just as the originator of a *ringi* proposal will generally not submit it formally until he is fairly sure it will be received favorably, Japanese managers in general do not, like their foreign counterparts, hold formal meetings to discuss subjects and make decisions. They meet to formally agree on what has already been decided in informal discussions behind the scene.

These informal discussions are called *nemawashi* (nay-mah-wah-she), which literally means, "make sure the roots grow."

Nemawashi protocol does not require that all managers who might be concerned be consulted. But agreement must always be obtained from the "right" person—meaning the individual in the department, division or upper echelon of the company management who really exercises power.

Kaigi
Talk Meets

Since business management in Japan is more of a consensus process, Japanese managers probably have more meetings, *kaigi* (kie-ghee), than their counterparts in the West. Some standard ones:

Torishimariyakukai	Board of Directors' Meeting
Jūyakukai	Directors' Meeting
Buchō-kai	Department Heads' Meeting
I-in-kai	Committee Meeting

Jūyaku ga Nai
"No Executives" in Japan

One authority on Japanese management makes the rather astounding observation that while there are "business managers" in Japan, there are no "business executives" in the Western sense. Masaaki Imai, Managing Director of Cambridge Research Institute-Japan says that in a situation where employment is permanent and management is collective, there can be "no such thing" as an executive.

Imai explains: "In a way, every (white collar employee) in a company is an executive, and everyone is not. When a university graduate joins a company, he knows that some 13 to 15 years later he will be promoted to *ka-chō* (section chief), even if his first assignment is clipping newspapers. So do all of his colleagues who joined the company when he did.

"Thus from the standpoint of the individual, the transition from employee to 'executive' is automatic. Until he is promoted to *ka-chō* level, he belongs to the union and makes such demands as pay raises to the management. One morning he wakes up to find that he has become *ka-chō*, and starts dealing with the union on behalf of the company . . .

". . . Whether a Japanese is an executive or not is not so much derived from his own will and effort, but from the years he has spent in the company." Imai adds that many companies often reserve important management positions for union leaders for the day they stop being union leaders. (In Japan, most unions are 'company unions' as opposed to craft or trade unions.)

The role of *Jūyaku* (Jew-yah-coo) or "Big Executives" in typical, large Japanese companies is also quite different from that in comparable American companies. Most major Japanese firms select the members of their Board of Directors, *Torishimariyakkai* (Toe-ree-she-mah-ree-yaak-kie), from within their own company. The boards are typically made up of the president of the particular company, and other line executives down to department heads. The function of the board is therefore mostly ceremonial, and the title primarily "social."

The board that really "runs" the large Japanese company—if one does—is the *Jōmukai* (Joe-moo-kie) or Managing Directors' Board. This board is made up of the heads of key departments, with the president as chairman. Most *Jōmukai* are often little more than "rubber stamp" boards dominated by one man, because the *sempai-kōhai* or senior-junior system invariably prevails.

Hanko
Chopping People Down

The Japanese have traditionally used *hanko* (name stamp, seal or "chop") in lieu of written signatures when signing contracts and other types of formal or official documents. Especially where government bureaus and agencies are concerned, up to a dozen or so men in as many departments may be required to stamp a document, sometimes several times each in different places.

The mechanics of the practice by itself are irksome, often to an extreme degree, but it is usually something that time and great patience can surmount—if no hitches develop. Among the problems that can and do develop regularly: one (or more) of the men whose stamp is required is not available and following their hierarchical habit of grading everything, the name seals may have to go on in a prescribed order, causing long delays; someone decides he is not going to cooperate because he disapproves of the document, the person who originated it, or because he may be feuding with some of the other managers, etc.

Foreign businessmen living and working in Japan have the right to get a *hanko* stamp made and, if it is registered, use it as their legal signature. But few go to the trouble since the foreigner is allowed to write out his name—although in some cases the signing has to be certified before it is legal. Also, the *hanko* present a security problem since they can bind their owners to a contract even if affixed without their knowledge or authorization.

While written signatures are now the rule in international business in Japan, the *hanko* is still something to be reckoned with in dealings within the confines of Japanese companies and with government agencies, and is likely to remain so for some time.

Mibun
The Rights Have It

Everybody in Japan has his or her *mibun* (me-boon) and every *bun* has its special rights and responsibilities. There are special rights and special restrictions applying to managers only, to students only, to teachers only, to workers only, etc. The restrictions of a particular category are usually clearcut and are intended to control the behavior of the people within their categories at *all* times—the office employee even when he is not working, the student when he isn't in school.

The traditional purpose of the feudalistic *mibun* concept was to maintain harmony within and between different categories of people. A second purpose was to prevent anyone from bringing discredit or shame upon his category or his employer.

A good example of the *mibun* system at work was once told by Konosuke Matsushita, founder of the huge Matsushita Electric Company. At the age of 10, Matsushita was apprenticed in a bicycle shop, which meant that he was practically a slave, forced to work from five in the morning until bedtime.

In addition to his regular duties, Matsushita had to run to a tobacco store several times a day for customers who came into the shop. Before he could go, however, he had to wash. After several months of this, he hit upon the idea of buying several packs of cigarettes at one time, with his own money, so that when a customer asked for tobacco he not only could hand it to him immediately but profit a few *sen* on each pack, since he received a discount by buying 20 packs at a time.

This not only pleased the bicycle shop customers but also Matsushita's master, who complimented him highly on his ingenuity. A few days later, however, the master of the shop told him that all the other workers were complaining about his enterprise and that he would have to stop it and return to the old system.

It was not within the *bun* of a mere flunky to demonstrate such ability.

The aims of foreign businessmen are often thwarted because they attempt to get things done by Japanese whose *bun* does not allow them to do whatever is necessary to accomplish the desired result. Instead of telling the businessmen they can't do it, or passing the matter on to someone who can, there is a tendency for the individual to wait a certain period, or until they are again approached by the businessmen, then announce that it is impossible.

In any dealings with a Japanese company it is especially important to know the *bun* of the people representing the firm. The Japanese businessman who does have individual authority is often buttressed behind subordinates whose *bun* are strictly limited. If the outsider isn't careful, a great deal of time can be wasted on the wrong person.

It is the special freedoms or "rights" of the *bun* system that cause the most trouble. As is natural everywhere, the Japanese minimize the responsibilities of their *bun* and emphasize the rights, with the result that there are detailed and well-known rules outlining the rights of each category, but few rules covering the responsibilities.

As one disillusioned bureaucrat-turned-critic put it, "The rights of government and company bureaucrats tend to be limitless, while responsibilities are ignored or passed on to underlings. The underlings in turn say they are powerless to act without orders from above—or that it isn't their responsibility." The same critic also said that the only ability necessary to become a bureaucrat was the ability to escape responsibility without being criticized.

A story related by a former editor of one of Japan's better known intellectual magazines illustrates how the *mibun* system penetrates into private life. While still an editor with the magazine, Mr. S. went out drinking one night with a very close writer-friend. While they were drinking, another writer, the noted Mr. D., came into the bar and joined them.

Mr. S continues: "I was not 'in charge' of Mr. D. in my publishing house and didn't know him very well, but according to Japanese business etiquette I should have bowed to him, paid him all kinds of high compliments and told him how much I was obligated to him. But it was long after my working hours and I was enjoying a drink with a friend who was also a writer, so I just bowed and paid little attention to him."

"At this, Mr. D. became angry and commanded me in a loud voice to go home. I refused to move and he began shouting curses at me. I shouted back at him that I was drinking with a friend and it was none of his business, but he continued to abuse me loudly until my friend finally managed to quiet him down. Of course, I would have been fired the next day except that my friend was able to keep Mr. D. from telling the directors of my company."

In doing business with a Japanese company, it is important to find out the rank of each individual you deal with so you can determine the extent of his *bun*. It is also vital that you know the status of his particular section or department, which has its own rank within the company.

There are other management characteristics that make it especially difficult for the uninitiated foreigner to deal with a Japanese company, including barriers to fast, efficient communication between levels of management within the company. Everything must go through the proper chain-of-command, in a carefully prescribed, ritualistic way. If any link in this vertical chain is missing—away on business or sick—routine communication usually stops there. The ranking system does not allow Japanese managers to delegate authority or responsibility to any important extent. Generally, one person cannot speak for another.

Hisho-Kan
Where Are All the Secretaries?

As most Western businessmen would readily admit, they simply could not get along without their secretaries. In many ways, secretaries are as important, if not more so, than the executives themselves. In Japan only the rare businessman has a secretary whose role even approximates the function of the Western secretary.

The reason for the scarcity of secretaries in Japan is manyfold. The style of Japanese management—the collective work-groups, decision-making by consensus, face-to-face communication, and the role of the manager as harmony-keeper instead of director—practically precludes the secretarial function. Another factor is the language itself, and the different language levels demanded by the subordinate/superior system. Japanese does not lend itself to clear, precise instructions. It cannot be transcribed easily or quickly, either in short-hand or by typewriter. As a result, the Japanese are not prepared, psychologically or practically, for doing business through secretaries.

The closest the typical Japanese company has to secretaries in the American sense are receptionists; usually pretty, young girls who are stationed at desks in building lobbies and in central floor and hall areas. They announce visitors who arrive with appointments, and try to direct people who come in on business without specific appointments to the right section or department. When a caller who has never had any business with the company, and has no appointment, appears at one of the reception desks, the girl usually tries to line him up with someone in the General Affairs *(Sōmu-Bu)* Department.

Smaller Japanese companies and many departments in larger companies do not have receptionists. In such cases, no specific individual is responsible for greeting and taking care of callers. The desks nearest the door are usually occupied by the lowest ranking members in the department, and it is up to the caller to get the attention of one of them and make his business known.

Shigoto
It's Not the Slot

The importance of face-to-face meetings in the conduct of business in Japan has already been mentioned. Regular personal contact is also essential in maintaining "established relations" (the ability to *amaeru*) with business contacts. The longer two people have known each other and the more often they personally meet, the firmer this relationship.

This points up a particular handicap many foreign companies operating in Japan inadvertently impose on themselves by switching their personnel every two, three or four years. In the normal course of business in Japan, it takes at least two and sometimes as many as five years before the Japanese begin to feel like they really know their foreign employer, supplier, client or colleague.

It also generally takes the foreign businessman transferred to Japan anywhere from one to three or so years to learn enough to really become effective in his job. Shortly afterward, he is transferred, recalled to the head office, is fired, or quits, and is replaced by someone else.

American businessmen in particular tend to pay too little attention to the disruption caused by personnel turnover, apparently because they think more in terms of the "position" or the "slot" being filled by a "body" that has whatever qualifications the job calls for. Generally speaking, they play down the personality of the person filling the position, and often do not adequately concern themselves with the role of human relations in business.

This, of course, is just the opposite of the Japanese way of doing things, and accounts for a great deal of the friction that develops between Japanese and Westerners in business matters.

Tsūshin
Don't Call Me...

One of the most common complaints about Japanese companies is that they often fail to answer business inquiries or requests for information. There are, of course, two sides to the story, Many Japanese companies receive hundreds of inquiries every week from all over the world. Some of the inquiries are from large, reputable firms; others are from small companies trying to get started, from retail shops, and even individuals. The letters from abroad are mostly in English—but they also come in such languages as Urdu, Swahili, Tagalog and Tamil.

Imagine, if you will, how many American, British or French companies receiving dozens of letters from unknown sources, and frequently in rare languages, would bother to do anything with them. But over and above this consideration, there are several reasons why written inquiries to Japanese companies are often not answered.

The individual Japanese section or department manager generally does not have a secretary or even a "pool" typist to take care of correspondence. Inquiries coming from abroad, unless they are addressed to a specific individual in a section or department, most likely go to the General Affairs Department, where they tend to end up in the hands of young clerks still undergoing on-the-job-training.

Besides this, it is not customary for Japanese companies to indiscriminately provide information about their products or services to unknown outsiders (except for making catalogs or flyers available on special occasions). The reaction tends to be, "Who wants to know, and why?"

Another factor that works against Japanese companies "automatically" answering inquiries from unknown parties is that individual managers, and certainly not clerks, generally do not have the authority to provide information or make offers on their own. The Japanese manager can say "no"—or do nothing, which is the same thing—especially if he doesn't refer the request or proposition to someone else—but he cannot expose the company or commit the company to anything by himself.

The tendency of Japanese companies to be closed-mouthed—even secretive—about their business is a result of several factors, cultural and economic. Japanese society has traditionally been closed—made up of exclusive groups and groups within groups; each one very sensitive about its existence, responsibilities and privileges, basically hostile to all other groups, and to some degree in competition with them.

This system, and the ethics responsible for its development, precludes the free and open exchange of information between groups, since a primary motivation is to protect one's own integrity and out-do all other related groups. This attitude and practice still prevails to a formidable degree in Japan's business world today.

Of course there are exceptions, since there are over 4,000 trading companies in Japan whose primary function is engaging in international business, and a significant percentage of the country's major manufacturers have their own export departments. But the fact remains that the

Japanese do not like to do business by mail. Their system gives precedence to and often makes mandatory the face-to-face meeting and the development of a personal relationship before any business transpires.

Yakusoku
"On My Word"

Japanese businessmen generally do all they can to avoid getting involved with the law and courts. In the past, it was customary in Japan for both parties in a dispute to be regarded as equally guilty. "Justice" was often both harsh and expensive, and under any circumstances it was usually wise to avoid bringing one's self to the attention of the authorities.

In Japan today the law is still regarded as a costly and complicating process. The American tendency to bring in lawyers on business negotiations and to draw up minutely detailed contracts can be very upsetting to the Japanese. They prefer general agreements that allow the parties to discuss and negotiate particular points as they come up, leaving both sides a great deal more flexibility.

The Japanese businessmen's credo is that every effort should be made to avoid problems by cooperating on an individual and personal as well as company and industry level, and when problems do arise they should be solved by arbitration and compromise. Their view is that since it is impossible to know exactly what is going to happen in the future, detailed, written contracts are bound to become obsolete.

In days past, there were few written contracts in Japan. They depended instead on *yakusoku* (yah-coo-so-coo) or "verbal agreements," with the parties bound to each other by goodwill and obligation. When such agreements were reached and were of some importance, they were usually marked by a drinking party and the ceremonial clapping of hands a prescribed number of times in a particular cadence.

While disliking and distrusting written contracts, Japanese businessmen recognize that they have little or no choice but to use them in their international business. They are especially sensitive to the fact that they usually do not know their foreign "partners" very well, cannot *amaeru* with them in full confidence and trust, and cannot depend on dealing with the same individuals from one day to the next, much less for year after year.

Sekininsha
Finding Where the Buck Stops

In Western companies there is almost always one man who has final responsibility and authority, and it is easy to identify this man. All you have to do is ask, "Who is in charge?"

In Japanese companies, no one individual is in charge. Both responsibility and authority are dispersed among the managers as a group. The larger the company, the more people are involved. When there are mistakes or failures, Japanese management does not try to single out the individual at fault. They try to focus on the cause of the failing, in an effort to find out why it happened. In this way, the man who made the mistake does not lose face, and all concerned have an opportunity to learn a lesson.

Ranking Japanese businessmen advise that it is in fact difficult to determine who has real authority and who makes final decisions in a Japanese company. Said a Sony director: "Even a top executive must consult his colleagues before he 'makes' a decision because he has become a high executive more by his seniority than his leadership ability. To keep harmony in his company he must act as a member of a family." Sony's Morita predicts that, because of this factor, the traditional concept of promotion by seniority cannot have much of a future in Japan. He agrees, however, that it is not something that can be changed in a short period of time.

In approaching a Japanese company about a business matter, it is therefore almost always necessary to meet and talk with the heads of several sections and departments on different occasions. After having gone through this procedure, you may still not get a clear-cut response from anyone, particularly if the various managers you approached have not come to a favorable consensus among themselves. It is often left up to you to synthesize the individual responses you receive and draw your own conclusions.

It is always important and often absolutely essential that the outsider (foreign or Japanese) starting a new business relationship with a Japanese company establish good rapport with each level of management in the company. Only by doing so can the outsider be sure his side of the story, his needs and expectations, will get across to all the necessary management levels.

Earle Okumura (Okumura and Wilking, Los Angeles-based consultants), one of a growing number of Americans who are expert in doing business in Japan, suggests the following procedure in establishing "lines of communication" with a Japanese company when the project concerns the introduction of new technology to be used by the Japanese firm:

Step I—Ask a director or the head of the Research & Development Department to introduce you to the *kachō* (section head) who is going to be directly "in charge" of your project within his department. Take the time to develop a personal relationship with the *kachō* (eating and drinking with him, etc.), then ask him to tell you exactly what you should do, and how you should go about trying to achieve and maintain the best possible working relationship with the company.

Step II—Ask the R&D *kachō*, with whom you now have at least the beginnings of an *amae* relationship, to introduce you to his counterparts in the Production, Quality Control and Sales Departments, etc., and go through the same get-acquainted process with each of them, telling them all about yourself, your company and your responsibilities. In all of these contacts, care must be taken not to pose any kind of a threat or embarrassment to the different *kachō*.

Step III—After you have established a good, working relationship with the various *kachō* concerned, thoroughly explained your side of the project and gained an understanding of their thinking, responsibilities and capabilities, the third step is to get an appointment with the president or managing director of the company for a relaxed, casual conversation about policies, how much you appreciate being able to work with the company, and the advantages that should accrue to both parties as a result of the joint venture.

Do not, Okumura cautions, get involved in trying to pursue details of the project with the president or managing director. They will most likely not be familiar with them, and in any event will be more concerned about your reliability, sincerity and ability to deal with their company.

Before an American businessman commits himself to doing business with another company, he checks out the company's assets, technology, financial stability, etc. The Japanese businessman is first interested in the character and quality of the people in the other company, and secondarily interested in its facilities and finances. The Japanese put more stock in goodwill and the quality of the interpersonal relationships in their business dealings.

Mizu Shōbai
The "Water" Business

Mizu shōbai (Me-zoo show-bye), literally "water business," is a euphemism for the so-called entertainment trades—which is a euphemism for the hundreds of thousands of bars, cabarets, clubs, Turkish bathhouses, hotspring spas and Geisha "houses" that flourish in Japan. The term *mizu* is applied to this area of Japanese life because, like pleasure, water sparkles and soothes, then goes down the drain or evaporates into the air. *Shōbai* or "business" is a very appropriate word, because the *mizu shōbai* is one of the biggest businesses in Japan, employing some five million men and women.*

Drinking and enjoying the companionship of attractive young women in *mizu shōbai* establishments is an important part of the lives of Japanese businessmen. There are basically two reasons for their regular drinking. First, ritualistic drinking developed into an integral part of religious life in ancient times, and from there was carried over into social and business life.

Thus, for centuries, no formal function or business agreement of any kind has been complete without a drinking party to mark the occasion. At such times, drinking is more of a duty than anything else. Only a person who cannot drink because of some physical condition or illness is normally excused.

The second reason for the volume of customized drinking that goes on in Japan is related to the distinctive subordinate/superior relationships between people, and the minutely prescribed etiquette that prevents the Japanese from being completely informal and frank with each other *except when they are drinking.*

Because the Japanese must be so circumspect in their behavior at all "normal" times, they believe it is impossible to really get to know a person without drinking with him. The sober person, they say, will always hold back and not reveal his true character. They feel ill-at-ease with anyone who refuses to drink with them at a party or outing. They feel that refusing to drink indicates a person is arrogant, excessively proud and unfriendly. The ultimate expression of goodwill, trust and humility is to drink to drunkenness with your co-workers and with close or important business associates in general. Those who choose for any reason not to go all the way, must simulate drunkenness in order to fulfill the requirements of the custom.

---

*For more on the subject of the *Mizu Shōbai*, see the author's *Bachelor's Japan* and *Businessman's After Hours Guide to Japan*.

Enjoying the companionship of pretty, young women has long been a universal prerogative of successful men everywhere. In Japan it often goes further than that. It has traditionally been used as an inducement as well as to seal bargains, probably because it is regarded as the most intimate activity men can share.

When the Japanese businessman offers his Western guest or client intimate access to the charms of pretty, young women—something that still happens regularly—he is not "pandering" or engaging in any other "nasty" practice. He is merely offering the Western businessman a form of hospitality that has been popular in Japan since ancient times. In short, Japanese businessmen do openly and without guilt feelings, what many Western businessmen do furtively.

The foreign businessman who "passes" when offered the opportunity to indulge in this custom, either before or after a bargain is struck, may be regarded as foolish or prudish for letting the opportunity go by, but he is no longer likely to be accused of insincerity.

Many Westerners find it difficult to join in wholeheartedly at the round of parties typically held for them by their Japanese hosts, especially if it is nothing more than a drinking party at a bar or club. Westerners have been conditioned to intersperse their drinking with jokes, boasting and long-winded opinions—supposedly rational—on religion, politics, business or what-have-you.

Japanese businessmen, on the other hand, do not go to bars or clubs at night to have serious discussions. They go there to relax emotionally and physically—to let it all hang out. They joke, laugh, sing, dance, and make short, rapid-fire comments about work, their superiors, personal problems and so on; but no long, deep discussions.

When the otherwise reserved and carefully controlled Japanese businessman does relax in a bar, cabaret or at a drinking party, he often acts—from a Western viewpoint—like a high school kid in his "cups" for the first time.

At a reception given by a group of American dignitaries at one of Tokyo's leading hotels, my table partner was the chief of the research division of the Japanese firm being honored. The normally sober and distinguished scientist had had a few too many by the time the speeches began, and was soon acting in the characteristic manner of the drunk. All during the speeches he giggled, sang, burped and whooped it up, much to the embarrassment of both sides.

In recent years, inflation has dimmed some of the nightly glow from Geisha houses, the great cabarets, the bars and the inn-restaurants in Japan's major cities. The feeling is also growing that the several billion dollars spent each year in the *mizu shōbai* is incompatible with Japan's present-day needs.

But like so many other aspects of Japanese life, the *mizu shōbai* is deeply embedded in the overall socio-economic system, as well as in the national psyche. It is not about to disappear in the foreseeable future.

Most of the money spent in the *mizu shōbai* comes from the so-called *Shayōzoku* (Shah-yoe-zoe-coo), "Expense-Account Tribe"—the large number of salesmen, managers and executives who are authorized to entertain clients, prospects and guests at company expense. Japanese companies are permitted a substantial tax write-off for entertainment purposes to begin with, and most go way beyond the legal limit (based on their capital), according to both official and unofficial sources.

Chapter 6

Nippongo
The Magnificent Barrier

Japlish
Smooth as a Baby's Ass

Some years ago, one of Japan's Big Three newspapers, with a circulation of over five million, carried an advertisement that was all in Japanese except for the headline. The headline read: "SMOOTH AS A BABY'S ASS."

The advertisement pointed up a language/communications problem that is apparently unique among the world's leading nations. Since every language is a mirror of the culture in which it developed, it is not surprising that the Japanese language reflects the psychology, the attitudes and the manners of the Japanese. In fact, as mentioned earlier, the Japanese language is the primary repository and transmitter of Japanese culture.

Japanese was a relatively adequate language as long as the Japanese dealt only with themselves and were able and content to maintain the character and style of their unique social system. Neither of these two conditions has existed for some time now, but the awkward tongue and centuries of machine-like conditioning still shackle the Japanese to their heritage.

There are three basic levels of the Japanese language: the "low" level used when addressing subordinates and some categories of younger persons; the "intimate" level used when conversing with family members and close friends of the same age; and an honorific or "high" level used when addressing superiors and respected elders.

Japanese etiquette demands that the proper level of language be used for every situation, and, of course, using either the common or low level of language to a superior is the worst possible breech of this deeply embedded social rule.

The tri-level character of the Japanese language, which grew out of their vertically structured social system, is one of the reasons why it is so difficult for the Japanese to talk to strangers. Until they find out the other person's social/business rank, they are very nearly tongue-tied. The Japanese can in fact, if they know a foreign language, approach and talk to foreigners easier than they can to other Japanese, because they do not have to be concerned about the social level of the language they use.

The Japanese language thus owes its most distinctive characteristics to the fact that those using it must take the most extreme care not to insult or shame anyone. This also partly explains the remarkably polite manners of the Japanese in all their normal social contacts with each other (and in most cases with foreigners)—discounting boarding crowded subways and trains, shopping in department store, etc., as "normal" contact.

Both the language and etiquette, inseparably intertwined, are a reflection of the inherent desire of the Japanese to "obviate shame-causing situations"; to prevent insults. The language is almost bare of curse words. The speaker who wants to flay someone has to depend upon manner of delivery rather than word-meaning. The only "curse" words that do exist are regularly heard on radio and television. Children playing in the street hurl them at each other and at adult passersby with complete abandon and without fear of being overly censored by their elders.

Once a Japanese has been shamed by the deliberate mis-use of language, whether he deserves the shame or not, he will react along perfectly predictable lines. He will become incensed and seek revenge which he must have if it takes the rest of his life. Or, if there is no possible way he can get back at the one who shamed him, he will become morbidly depressed and somehow inflict punishment on himself.

There are many Japanese today who are able to stand up under "verbal insults"—young people; salesmen; women in the entertainment trades. Others are also gradually discovering that they can escape the web that binds them to "the Japanese way." But their numbers are still relatively small. There are stories regularly in the daily newspapers recounting incidents of someone taking revenge—on someone else or himself—for being verbally shamed.

Very few foreigners, including long-time residents in Japan, speak Japanese. The vast majority of Japanese speak little or no English. The language barrier, coupled with other cultural differences relating to communication, causes more of the problems that constantly beset Japanese and Westerners doing business with each other than any other factor.

To give credit where it is due, the Japanese at least make an attempt to speak English. Most Western businessmen, however—especially high placed ones—consider learning Japanese too time-consuming, unnecessary, or beneath their dignity. Some who have been in Japan for years exhibit a perverse pride in their inability to speak the language, and regularly insult Japanese who fail to understand their comments or questions.

Almost all Japanese have studied English for anywhere from two to eight years, and will usually list English as something they have "accomplished." But, only a few can converse even halfway fluently in the language, or understand it when it is spoken to them. The reason for this is that their teachers in school could not speak English and therefore could not teach it as a spoken language. While a tremendous amount of effort was expended in "reading" English, it was read without benefit of knowing how to pronounce it. It thus comes out "Japanized."

The English word "bread" becomes "bu-re-do" when spoken or read by most Japanese. Similarly, "coming" becomes "ko-mi-n-gu." "Mr. Smith" becomes "Mi-s-ta Sumi-su," "girl" becomes "ga-ru" and so on.

The English that students are required to study by their teachers is often truly astounding. Innumerable times students have come to me and asked for help in translating an ordinary assignment. The selections they had been given were so esoteric, so stream-of-conscious vague, not one in a hundred native-born English speakers could have explained them in his own tongue!

Some of the wilder examples would shock the Western student if he should be called upon to render them into some foreign tongue, i.e. "The march of mankind is directed neither by his will, nor by his superstitions, but by the effect of his great and, as it were, accidental discoveries on his average nature. The discovery and exploitation of fire, of metals and gunpowder, of coal, steam, electricity, of flying machines, acting on human nature which is, practically speaking constant, molds the real shape of human life, under all the agreeable camouflage of religions, principles, policies and ideas. The comparisons with the effect of these discoveries and their unconscious influences of human life, the affect of political ideas is seen to be inconsiderable."*

Haji
Avoiding Shame

This situation is further complicated by a super-sensitive pride that often prevents the Japanese, once they attain professional status, from either admitting that their English is less than fluent or seeking help from someone who does

---

*Anthony Scarangello, *A Fulbright Teacher in Japan*, The Hokuseido Press, Tokyo, 1957. P. 123.

know the language to advise them or proofread their publications, signs, etc., that are supposed to be in English.

The answer to this paradox seems to be that as long as no one points out the errors to the people responsible, it is possible for them to assume there are no errors, so no "face" is lost. And, it is considered extremely impolite for anyone to point out such mistakes. Many times I have seriously embarrassed Japanese friends and co-workers by calling attention to flagrant and harmful errors in everything from menus to *White Papers* issued by one of the Ministries.

Larger Japanese firms generally have a number of employees who speak English quite well. Other firms usually have at least one or two who speak broken English, and with the aid of a dictionary can laboriously turn out letters in the language, and translate English language correspondence into Japanese.

These latter firms never completely understand all the things the foreign businessman says or writes to them, and as a result are almost always working in some degree of darkness. Even when information or instructions are given to a Japanese company in Japanese, the possibility of a misunderstanding, or failure to "get through," is enormous.

Because of both the inherent vagueness of the Japanese language and the distinctive attitudes and social behavior that continue to force the Japanese to use their language in a vague, esoteric manner, even well-educated, erudite people often have difficulty expressing themselves clearly. A Tokyo University professor whose specialty is communications estimates that on the first time around the Japanese are able to fully understand only about 85 percent of what they say to each other. It is common for Japanese to have to repeat themselves several times to get even simple concepts across. The language is so vague that in many ordinary conversations people frequently have to stop and trace one or more Chinese ideograms—usually with their finger on any surface handy or in the air—in order to communicate an idea. If the ideogram happens to be an unusual one, and there are hundreds of unusual ones, or a person has forgotten it or never learned it, he may never fully understand.

The Japanese language actually can be spoken much more directly and therefore much more effectively than it is by most Japanese, but for a Japanese to do so is regarded as a serious breach of etiquette. Foreigners who have a good command of the language are able to communicate ideas more quickly and more clearly than the Japanese, since they are not forced by habit or Japanese propriety to speak in esoteric circumlocutions. In doing so, however, they run the risk of seriously offending whoever they are talking to, so it is necessary for them to exercise caution.

Sukoshi Dekimasu
I Can Do a Little

A smattering of Japanese is easy to learn and will prevent many of the situations which cause basic problems for the foreigner in Japan. These usually are concerned with simple things like food, lodging, time, direction, etc., and require only a small vocabulary and little or no knowledge of grammar. A great many of the more common problems of communication occur in the first place because the foreigner assumes that any Japanese he encounters understands English.

I have watched visiting travelers and businessmen approach Japanese clerks, office personnel, policemen and others with questions, sometimes simple and sometimes complicated, as if it would be the most natural thing for them to understand English—and then be unbecomingly indignant when it turned out that they didn't.

Most people who have studied a foreign language can understand more of it than they can speak. In Japan it is usually just the opposite. The typical Japanese who has studied the language can generally say many things in English, if given the time to laboriously string the words together. This misleads foreigners into believing that everything they say is understood and they go on and on, and are sorely disappointed when the Japanese concerned fails to react as expected.

It seems to be customary for some foreigners to assume that raising their voices and getting angry will help them communicate with Japanese whose understanding of English is limited. They eventually find, however, that this does not achieve the desired result. It serves not only to further befuddle the Japanese; it also turns them into enemies who will never forget or forgive and one day, in some way, will take their revenge.

In many cases, it is difficult to immediately determine how much English an individual speaks or understands. The visiting businessman or traveler can avoid some of the complications that frequently arise in such situations by engaging the individual concerned in a bit of preliminary conversation to see how much he or she understands. If the topic is important, and the person's understanding seems doubtful, the best thing to do is write out what you have to say.

Foreign businessmen who receive letters from Japanese firms written in adequate English are also cautioned to remember that there is an excellent chance an answering letter will not be thoroughly understood. This is not always because of inability on the part of the Japanese. I have examined more than a thousand letters from foreign firms to Japanese companies and found some completely incomprehensible. Many others were so general or so cryptic that much of the meaning was obscured.

Besides a language barrier that makes communications between Japanese and Westerners difficult, there are other cultural factors that hinder the Japanese in their relations with outsiders. For several generations, the Japanese were taught to repress their emotions in public; to display no curiosity, surprise, displeasure or pain in the presence of a superior, and to obey all orders without question.

Still today in the educational system in Japan there is very little student participation. There is little or no discussion in class. One of the results of this system is that the average Japanese has a difficult time responding to blunt questions, and also finds it hard to express his feelings verbally with anywhere near the amount of enthusiasm expected by Americans, for example.

The Japanese are well aware that their language is difficult; that it has its limitations as an effective means of communication. At the same time they have traditionally regarded their unique language as an important line of defense against foreign intrusion, spying or snooping, not only in the political and diplomatic spheres but also economically and socially.

Wakarimasu Ka?
Getting Through

Over the generations, so few Westerners have mastered the Japanese language that the Japanese came to more or less believe that it couldn't be learned by Europeans, and that its impenetrability provided them with a protective cloak of inestimable value. As a result of this attitude, the Japanese have always been more than willing to at least try to learn foreign languages, and continue to be amazed, even shocked, when confronted by a foreigner who speaks their language.

The Japanese also continue to be extraordinarily sensitive to racial differences. To hear their own language coming out of a foreigner's mouth, especially when the foreigner is Caucasian or black, is a surprise that often has rather startling consequences. The image of Japanese-speaking foreigners is so remote from their minds, it often happens that a Westerner will say something to a Japanese in fluent Japanese and fail to be understood—because they were not mentally tuned to "receive" in their own language.

An American lawyer who conducts cases in Japanese once walked up to a policeman in downtown Tokyo and asked him in Japanese if he knew the whereabouts of an address in the area. The policeman looked uncomfortable for several seconds, then blurted out: "I no speak English!" This peeved the lawyer and he proceeded to lecture the unfortunate cop in such a loud voice that a crowd gathered.

The lawyer could probably have saved himself a lot of bother and the police officer a lot of embarrassment if he had remembered to preface his question with one of the several conversational openers which the Japanese customarily use and which, when a foreigner is concerned, serve to let the Japanese know that you are going to speak in Japanese and that they should get set to receive in their own language.

If one knows how to bow properly, it is often possible to bow and get the same message across. But this takes more skill and experience than what might be expected. The most effective method is to combine a bow with one of the commonly used polite prefaces. On occasion this doesn't work either, so there is no choice but to repeat yourself.

The linguistic weaknesses of the Japanese—coupled with their characteristic reluctance to admit to this weakness—is, of course, responsible for the strange and sometimes hilarious English-language advertising they do, especially when the ads are prepared by the company's own advertising department.

Tsūyaku
"Thinking," Not Just Words

Foreign businessmen have often related how they spent hour upon hour trying to get something important (to them) across to their Japanese counterpart, only to find their efforts wasted and the Japanese probably thinking they are "blithering idiots." One such American recently recounting an experience along this line, summed up the crux of the problem very aptly when he described the kind of interpreter that is needed when talking with or negotiating with Japanese businessmen. He said, "You need someone who can interpret thinking, not just words."

This same businessman also brought out another facet of Japanese social and business etiquette that often contributes to misunderstandings, friction and delays in Japanese/Western business relations. In his case, he had as an interpreter a young Japanese who had lived for many years in the United States and was quite fluent in English. Believing that having such a qualified interpreter gave him an opportunity to get all of his ideas across to his Japanese counterpart, he spent a number of hours carefully and precisely explaining his whole business philosophy, how he felt that business could and should be operated.

When he returned to his hotel he was thoroughly satisfied that he had finally penetrated the barrier. But he congratulated himself too soon. Shortly afterward he received a telephone call from the interpreter who apologized, saying that he had not translated most of the foreign businessman's comments because they would have "offended" the Japanese. The Western businessman's remarks, it seems, were mostly critical of the way the Japanese do business.

It is a serious breach of etiquette in Japan to criticize someone directly in public, even when the relationship is superior-to-subordinate; just as it has traditionally been "wrong" to disagree with people in public, or to be right when they are in error.

This social custom often forces intelligent people to appear foolish—or stupid—or indifferent, but it is an important means of avoiding behavior that others, both in inferior and superior positions, consider insulting. There are historical examples in Japan in which people forefeited their lives by publicly correcting or criticizing someone. Revenge for this type of "insult" today usually does not involve violence (except sometimes in the case of hoodlums), but it is often vicious in a subtle way. The Western businessman should be aware of this extraordinary sensitivity of the Japanese, and conduct himself accordingly.

One way of reducing possible friction in this area is for the Western businessman to explain that besides being unfamiliar with Japanese customs, the policies and practices of his own company which he cannot arbitrarily change make it impossible for him to conform completely to the *Japanese Way*. This is something like announcing to the Japanese, "I may insult you but I can't help it, and I apologize beforehand"—reasoning that is readily understandable in Japan.

A vital factor in the use of English-speaking Japanese interpreters by foreign businessmen in Japan is that most of the interpreters *are* young, often have had little or no business experience themselves, are likely to be inadequately experienced in handling human relations problems (which is always a big part of interpreting), and are almost always called upon to interpret to older, higher ranking Japanese executives.

In their efforts to use the proper level of polite speech to higher ranking individuals, young, inexperienced interpreters often confuse the meaning of what they are trying to say.

Because of this problem, it may be wiser for the foreign businessman to employ older persons as interpreters—even when their English language proficiency may be less than that of the recent university graduate (who may have studied abroad). The greater social status of the older individual will often more than compensate for a lesser ability in English.

If the foreign businessman wants to further balance the scales in his favor by engaging the services of an older man of recognized high social and economic rank, he should explain to the man of rank that his high status, knowledge and experience is needed to offset the foreigner's lack of understanding of local customs, etc.

Gaijin Kusai
Smelling Like a Foreigner

Foreign businessmen commonly assume that a Western-educated Japanese employee, interpreter, friend or contact who speaks adequate if not fluent English is a "friend" in an "enemy camp" who can be depended upon to carry out their orders and wishes fully. While each case has to be considered individaully, this is generally not so. There are a number of interesting reasons why it is not so.

First and most important, if the Western-educated Japanese is in a medium-sized or large organization, and especially if he is not one of the top executives, he is up against a system that constitutes the very soul of the Japanese, and despite his foreign veneer he is still very much a part of that system.

The Japanese are inexpressibly sensitive and proud, and if a co-worker should appear to flaunt his Western learning gained by actually living in the outside world, he takes a chance of being ostracized and forever relegated to the background in some meaningless position.

I have many times seen how difficult it is for Japanese who have studied overseas to get themselves back into the system and maintain friendly relations with other Japanese co-workers. They must exercise extreme care not to arouse the jealousy or ire of their fellow employees. Companies, of course, send their own employees abroad, but not until they have been fully indoctrinated in the company spirit and philosophy.

Many major Japanese companies still today have a more or less set policy against hiring anyone who has studied abroad. Their attitude is based on the sure knowledge that the individual who studies abroad invariably loses some of his Japaneseness and takes on what to "pure" Japanese are very noticeable Western manners and attitudes, and therefore becomes a round ball in a square hole —even though "better qualified" than other members of the firm. In earlier years, such returned students were often described as *Gaijin kusai* (Guy-gene-coo-sie), "Smelling like a foreigner."

During several years of living in Tokyo, I interviewed dozens of Japanese in their middle and late twenties who had studied overseas for extended periods, and could not get a job with a major Japanese firm because they happened to be without very powerful personal connections. Others I know of who were able to get a job had to be content with positions in which their abilities, especially in English, were not used.

The companies concerned prefer to continue using Japanese employees who have studied only in Japan even though they are capable only of writing and speaking a sort of pidgin English. They explain the policy by claiming that the Japanese who become Westernized are no longer emotionally or intellectually capable of fitting into the unique Japanese company system. Since it is absolutely necessary for many Japanese firms to have employees who can read, write and speak foreign languages well, some companies do make the "sacrifice" and employ people who have studied overseas.

The foreign-educated Japanese employee thus tends to become a buffer between foreigners and his firm. When he speaks to the foreigner he puts on his Western veneer and understands and sympathizes with the foreigner. When he turns around and speaks to his Japanese associates the system demands that he become one of them and do his best to see the foreigner through their "Japanese" eyes.

Makoto
Sincerity Japanese Style

It is not unusual for both Japanese and Western businessmen to accuse each other of being insincere—and sometimes dishonest. What neither side appreciates is that in most cases they are referring to entirely different concepts of sincerity and honesty. In many situations, the Japanese idea of right and wrong is quite different from the Western idea. To the typical Japanese, right or wrong is not so much based on an unvarying, universal code of ethics or principles, as upon time, place, the people involved, and other circumstances. The Japanese concept of justice is subsequently not as abstract as the Western idea.

I once attended a large reception staged in Tokyo by the importing division of an American company for Hitachi Ltd., one of their suppliers, and several guests of note. There were a number of speeches by Hitachi executives, and in every case each speaker not only began and ended his talk with an appeal for the Americans to be sincere in their dealings with them, but also harped on this point throughout his speech.

Catching the spirit of the thing, some of the American speakers countered and asked the Japanese to also be sincere, in what an outsider would probably have thought were spontaneous demonstrations of goodwill in which both parties were talking about the same thing and were really communicating with each other. But sincerity as used by the Japanese has altogether a different meaning than it does to Westerners. And it is of course vitally important to know this difference when doing business with Japanese.

Sincerity to most Westerners means free from pretense or deceit; in other words, honest and truthful without reservations. But to the typical Japanese, being *makoto* (mah-coe-toe), means to properly discharge all of one's obligations so that everything will flow smoothly; so that harmony will be maintained. It also means being careful not to say anything or do anything that would cause loss of face. By extension, it further means that the *makoto* person will not be self-seeking, will not get excited or provoke others to excitement (unless he wants to be attacked!), will not reveal his innermost thoughts, will not, in fact, do anything that is disruptive.

This, obviously, does not necessarily include or require strict adherence to what Westerners like to call "honesty" and "frankness," since harmony of a kind can be maintained indefinitely as long as both sides play according to the same rules. And the Japanese, just like Westerners, tend to think and behave as if their rules were the ones being used.

The Japanese businessman, as mentioned earlier, often seems to be more concerned with form and manner than he is with the end results of any effort—although results are of course important to him. Since this attitude is nearly opposite typical Western thinking, it naturally causes varying degrees of misunderstanding and friction between the parties involved.

Japanese still tend to think in terms of personal relationships and subjective circumstances in their business dealings. Thus an agreement between a Japanese and a foreign businessman should be reduced to its basic elements, and each point thoroughly discussed, to make sure each side understands and actually does agree to what the other side is saying.

Chapter 7

Yamato Damashii
The Spirit of Japan

Ware Ware Nippon-Jin
"We Japanese!"

For centuries the Japanese have "described" their unique spirit and character as *Yamato Damashii* (Yah-mah-toe Dah-mah-shee). *Yamato* is written with ideograms that mean "Great Peace," and is the old word for "Japan." *Damashii* means "heart" or "soul." Put together, they refer to the traditional spirit and personality of the Japanese in much the same way that "Puritan Ethic" is sometimes used in reference to characteristics of certain categories of Americans.

The use of the word *Yamato* in this context is significant because it emphasizes the traditional Japanese preoccupation with peace and harmony. Of course, this is "Japanese" peace and harmony, according to their values and definitions, and as expressed in the key words already discussed: *amae, on, giri, tsukiai*, etc. There are other important words and phrases that elaborate on the nuances of Japanese values, feelings, fears and aspirations:

Jibun Ga Nai
Life Without a "Self"

The Japanese, especially those born before 1945, tend to have shallow and fragile concepts of themselves as individual entities. There is a phrase used to express this feeling, *jibun ga nai* (jee-boon gah nie), "I have no self," which sociologists say is probably unique to the Japanese language.

It is not difficult, of course, to understand why this factor became an important aspect of the Japanese character. The traditional *Japanese Way* gave precedence in all things to the family and the group. Also, in virtually all instances, status and function were more important than the individual.

Just one of the ways this factor affects the foreign businessman in Japan or dealing with Japanese is graphically illustrated by a typical incident that took place recently. A foreign businessman resident in Tokyo took his two top Japanese assistants to the United States for a familiarization tour of his company's American operations. The Japanese executives had been with the Japan branch of the U.S. company for several years and, of course, knew the American resident director quite well.

During all the years the two Japanese managers had worked with the American businessman in Tokyo they never once called him by his first name. It was always "Mr. So & So." Within a day after the three men arrived in the U.S., however, the Japanese were calling their American employer by his given name. in an atmosphere of intimate friendliness and rapport that is so characteristic of American behavior.

"I thought," said the American businessman, "that we had finally achieved a break-thru in our relations—and that we would thereafter be on a much more satisfying level in both our business and personal relationships.

"But," he added, "much to my surprise and disappointment, no sooner were we back in Japan than these two fine gentlemen dropped the relaxed relationship we had developed while in the U.S., became rather stiff in their manners and began again calling me by my last name."

This incident emphasizes an extraordinary dilemma in Japanese society today. After centuries of repressing their emotions, their desires and even their spirits, for the sake of harmony in a meticulously prescribed hierarchically ranked social system, the Japanese lost much of the ability to exercise their own individuality.

This system of de-emphasizing the individual in favor of the group was further strengthened by giving the name of the clan, the place of residence, occupation and title precedence over the individual's name.

Still today the use of the given name is rare among adults in Japan. In business and the professions, the identity of the individual is usually blurred—or in some cases made virtually non-existent.

The individual becomes obscured somewhere in the shadows of his position or occupation, and is addressed by his title or function instead of his name. The president of a company is addressed as *"Shacho."* Department heads are called *"Bucho."* Teachers are referred to as *"Sensei"* (Sin-say-ee), "Teacher" or "Professor." The butcher is addressed as *"Nikuya-san"* (Nee-coo-yah-sahn) or "Mr. Meatman," and so on, resulting in one of the most inhibiting, limiting and painful, personal handicaps now facing the Japanese.

Having lived and worked in Japan for many years, I can personally testify to the damage this system does to the relationships between Japanese and non-Japanese, especially Americans.

I have had close relationships with many Japanese for more than 20 years but there is a deep psychological barrier that prevents me from feeling perfectly at ease with them *because I have to call them Mr. Yamaguchi, Mr. Kameda or Mr. Sato!*

It is hard to believe that this barrier can be so powerful, so disturbing; but it is and it cannot be denied.

This barrier does not exist just between Japanese and foreigners. It also exists between Japanese; and the pain, frustration, longing and loneliness it causes appears to be even more acute.

The Japanese are aware of the baleful influence of this out-moded, feudalistic and inhuman system, but it is so deeply rooted in their society they so far find it impossible to discard.

It is my belief that until the Japanese can succeed in eliminating this system and establishing their own personal identities by calling each other—and non-Japanese—by their given names they will continue to suffer poignant feelings of inadequacy and insecurity, and be at a serious disadvantage in their efforts to become full-fledged members of the world community.

Younger Japanese, and the older businessmen who have managed to become more individualistic in their attitudes and actions, are not nearly as "nameless" as the typical Japanese adult, but they nevertheless are severely restricted in their relationships with foreigners. It is difficult for them to react spontaneously and frankly to outsiders, although it is true that in almost every case not connected with business they make a genuine and generous effort.

Risshin Shusse
The Japanese Success-Drive

The extraordinary diligence and ambition of the Japanese is world-famous. What is not so well-known is exactly why the Japanese are so success-oriented. The mainspring of the seemingly frenetic drive of the Japanese—which appeared suddenly in full bloom in 1868 when the feudal system of government fell—is apparently a combination of several historical factors, including their self-image as a superior people, and the fact that ambition was suppressed in Japan from earliest times to the beginning of the modern industrial era.

During Japan's long feudal age, social class and occupations were hereditary. The only characteristics that were approved and rewarded were a dedication to hard work and loyalty to superiors within the rigid family and clan system.

With the fall of the feudal system in 1868, the new government began an intensive campaign to bring the country up to the industrial level of the U.S. and advanced European nations. Part of this campaign was an intense effort to imbue every child in the country with a concept of success known as *Risshin shusse*, (Rees-sheen Shus-say) or something like "Rise to eminence (in the world) through success!"

"*Shusse* success is distinctive in that it places major emphasis on the group instead of the individual," explains Hiroshi Hazama, professor of Industrial Sociology at the Tokyo University of Education. The success of the individual depends on the success of the group, beginning with the immediate work group and, by extension, going all the way up to include the whole country.

Prof. Hazama adds that *shusse* success is not measured in terms of wealth, but in social position. Social status is achieved by becoming a teacher, doctor, a businessman, etc. The apex of social status is to become the leader of one's group regardless of its size, and receive the coveted title of *chō*.

This title, with its accompanying social prestige rather than financial rewards, is the criterion of *shusse* success. Of course, the purity of this motive has suffered considerably in recent decades, since current life-styles make financial success an absolute necessity.

Hazama adds that the social status gained from being an employer is also of vital importance in the Japanese value system—a factor that contributes to the penchant of the Japanese to form their own companies, no matter how small or precarious.

Defeat in World War II had a profound effect on the attitudes of the Japanese toward success. The family system in which the father or ranking male member was the absolute master was abolished. The introduction of "American-style" democracy made everyone equal in the eyes of the law. Wartime destruction reduced the overwhelming majority to the same economic level—flat out poverty.

These new postwar conditions led to the rapid replacement of the *shusse* or family-group concept of success by that of personal success in terms of both social position and the accumulation of wealth. Titles were still of vital importance, but so was money. Besides the compulsion of the former affluent to regain their lost wealth, those who had never before known anything except poverty were free for the first time to better themselves.

Ki Ga Susumanai
100 Million Dissatisfied Spirits

Psychiatrist Takeo Doi says that the famous industriousness of the Japanese cannot be fully explained without reference to a condition known as *ki ga susumanai* (key-gah sue-sue-mah-nie), which means something like "my spirit is not satisfied."

Doi says the Japanese have been conditioned over the centuries to feel a profound sense of dissatisfaction and dis-ease until they finish whatever task they are embarked upon or whatever goal they have set for themselves. When the goal is a great one, or is limitless, Doi says there is no end to the dissatisfaction the Japanese feel, and therefore no end to their compulsion to work at a furious pace.

The *ki ga susumanai* factor would also seem to help explain the obsession the Japanese have with size and rank, and the compulsion they have to be number one in everything.

Ichiban To Biri
Feeling Superior and Inferior

One of the more significant obstacles to understanding between the Japanese and outsiders—whether businessmen, politicians or diplomats—is what might be called the "two-faced" aspect of the typical Japanese character.

Americans, Germans, the English and the French in particular have traditionally been afflicted with a very conspicuous superiority complex that is a distinctive facet of their national character.

The Japanese also harbor a superiority complex that is as strong if not stronger than that of most other nationalities. But in the case of the Japanese, their national character is far more complicated because they are also subject at the same time to an intense inferiority complex.

The core of the "traditional" Japanese superiority complex probably derived from the ancient mythological theme that Japan was created by divine beings and that the Japanese themselves, however indirectly, were descendants of these same superior creatures. (A concept, I might add, that has long since disappeared in post-Feudal generations).

In any event, this basic cultural concept of superiority gradually became stronger over the centuries because of unchallenged insular nationalism and an inbred life-style that was eventually refined to delicate perfection. Cultural historians say the idea gained further stature when the Mongols attempted to invade Japan in 1174 and again in 1180, and both times were routed by the "divine" intervention of one of Japan's seasonal typhoons.

Development of the feudalistic *Samurai* warrior code from the 11th to the 15th centuries added pride and a remarkable capacity for arrogance to the convictions of superiority that had been growing in the Japanese from the dawn of their history.

When the first Westerners began arriving in Japan in the 15th and 16th centuries, the Japanese became even more convinced of their superiority in all important social and cultural pursuits. To them, the Westerners looked and often behaved like half-wild beasts. They were large, hairy, often dirty, and in contrast to the exquisitely well-behaved Japanese, had the manners of uncivilized barbarians.

The Japanese subsequently developed considerable admiration for the technical and material accomplishments of Westerners, but they continued to regard themselves as superior to Americans and Europeans in matters of the spirit and heart.

The inferior side of the Japanese "face" no doubt had its origin in Japan's relationships with Korea and China, beginning around the 3rd century A.D. and lasting well beyond the 8th century. At the start of this period, Japan was divided into numerous competing clans with primitive lifestyles, while China was at the height of one of its greatest dynasties. The impact this cultural disparity had on the Japanese mind is still very much in evidence.

The big difference between Japan's relationship with China well over a millenium ago and with the West today is that the Japanese could at least identify with the Chinese racially and emotionally, thus lessening the trauma resulting from their inferior position.

In contrast, the typical Japanese today finds it difficult or impossible to identify with Caucasian Westerners. Not only does the Caucasian's appearance irrevocably separate him from the Japanese, but many of his attitudes and manners are alien and shocking to the Japanese.

At the same time, the Japanese continue to envy Americans and some Europeans for their living standards, their individualism, their social and economic freedoms; even for their size and light-colored skin. The Japanese thus feel both superior and inferior to Westerners at the same time, with considerably more passion than they regard other Orientals.

Probably the one thing in which the Japanese now take the greatest pride and which makes them feel the most superior to other people (since defeat in war shattered the belief of their spiritual superiority) is their "humanism." The Japanese have long tended to believe that their social attitudes and institutions are the most human of all, and at least until recent decades they were imbued with a deep cultural belief that it was their duty to spread their own native brand of humanism to all other people.

As the world well knows, the Japanese have now achieved technological and economic par with the leading countries of the West. This accomplishment has noticeably increased their feelings of superiority, but their feelings of inferiority remain a disrupting influence in their lives because it is an emotional thing now primarily related to racial characteristics that are absolute, and to the miniscule size and economic vulnerability of their country.

Among other things, their sense of inferiority gives the Japanese an overwhelming desire to catch and surpass all other countries, with the result that they are accused of being "too ambitious." During the 1960s and 70s, they came close to destroying both their health and environment for the sake of economic growth.

The Japanese will not be able to rid themselves of this feeling of inferiority until they learn a new set of practical and spiritual values which give them a new respect for the individual, his worth and his responsibilities. They must learn at the same time to accept differences in ideas, in people and in customs, without constantly comparing and measuring their traditional way of life against foreign standards.

As for the future influence of the superiority complex of the Japanese, it seems to me that just as the Romans of long ago, the Germans in more recent years, and now the Americans have had to accept the fact that they are not endowed with any special ability or divine right to be masters of the world, the Japanese must also purge themselves of this ancient, egoistic impulse.

On the personal, individual level, the Japanese—like most other nationalities—must recognize and accept the idea that on the average they are no better and no worse than other people, and that neither their inferiority nor their superiority feelings have any inherent, natural basis in fact.

Once rid of both of these false, misleading and dangerous assumptions, the Japanese will find themselves much more comfortable and effective in their international relationships.

Mono-No-Aware
Aesthetics in Business

The Japanese, like most Asians, were traditionally as concerned with emotional and spiritual things as they were with material things. This attitude led to the development of a culture in which aesthetics often took precedence over reason. Natural beauty, and things made of basic materials in a "natural" way, became objects of worship. Communing with nature through poetry and various aesthetic appreciation "cults" was an intimate part of every person's life.

Psychiatrist Doi says the Japanese preoccupation with aesthetics throughout their history was caused by their urge to *amaeru* with nature. Thus the appreciation practices involving flowers, the moon, snow and even the sounds of insects are, in Doi's view, direct manifestations of the *amae* factor in Japanese culture. Doi reasons that the innate hunger of the Japanese for *amae* is so strong it cannot be satisfied—because there is literally no way to re-merge mother and child or the individual adult and nature (the cosmos).

As usual, there are several key words in Japanese that pertain to the role of aesthetics and nature-communion in Japan. One is *mono-no-aware* (moe-no-no-ah-wah-ray), which refers to an extraordinary sensitivity to nature, to beauty, and the ability to merge one's identity with that of an object or mood, especially one that is tinged with recognition of the impermanence of all things.

Another, more commonly used word is *shibui* (she-boo-ee), which refers to beauty that is in perfect harmony with nature and has a tranquil effect upon the viewer.*
Then there is *sabi* (sah-bee), an attribute of beauty some-

---

*For a detailed discussion of the aesthetic practices of the Japanese, see the author's *Oriental Secrets of Graceful Living*, Wilshire Book Company, Los Angeles. Also available from the author, c/o Simpson-Doyle & Company.

times called "the rust of the ages"—moss on a rock or tree, wrinkles on the face of an aged man or woman, waste wood bleached grey. *Wābi* (wah-bee) denotes another aspect of beauty in the Japanese lexicon. It refers to materials that are the epitome of simplicity and austerity. *Yūgen* (you-gin), "mystery" or "subtlety" connotes a type of beauty, dear to the Japanese, that "lies modestly beneath the surface of things."

There are more such descriptive words, all providing an additional insight into the extraordinary role of aestheticism in the distinctive life-style developed by the Japanese; and all aimed at achieving a deep, satisfying sense of identity with nature.

At the same time, beauty was not all tranquil harmony to the Japanese. There was another side of aesthetics expressed in the term *iki* (ee-key), which suggests wit, flair, stylishness and sophistication. *Iki* beauty refers to objects as well as character, habits and personality of the individual. The person with *iki* is cool and smooth, and floats through life with *savoir faire*.

The tradition of communing with nature through practices elevated to the level of aesthetic cults has considerably waned among the younger generations in Japan, but enough of it remains that some aesthetic appreciation and artistic skill is considered essential to the complete individual.

On the business side, many companies offer employees free training in aesthetic pursuits such as flower-arranging, dancing and the tea ceremony. The older and more successful the businessman, the more he tends to concern himself with spiritual and emotional contentment obtained through either artistic or aesthetic activities. He may look down on, or at least feel sorry for, the executive who is too busy or too insensitive to do likewise.

Foreign businessmen who are serious about getting to know and establishing a lasting rapport with their Japanese counterparts, are well advised to also cultivate an appreciation for simple beauty and the myriad workings of nature.

Kanjō Wo Sasuru
Emotional Strokes

Japanese who have not been Westernized—and this means the majority—are generally ill-at-ease in the company of Westerners, even if they speak enough of a foreign language to communicate on a basic level. They simply have not been conditioned to engage in casual free-wheeling conversations with anyone except long-time Japanese friends.

Americans are often the most difficult for the Japanese to associate with. Our loose, back-slapping manner is exactly the type of behavior they were traditionally trained to avoid. As mentioned earlier, the penalty for breaching social etiquette in Feudal Japan was extremely serious, and in some cases carried the death sentence—a circumstance that helped make "proper" behavior second nature to the Japanese.

The Japanese, as of course do other societies, have a prescribed form and manner for every familiar situation that might arise. When a situation that is outside of their normal experience, and over which they have no control, does come up, they are at a loss for what to do, and undergo intense discomfort and embarrassment.

Most Japanese, as much as they might like to, cannot become close to a foreigner and cannot enjoy a mutually satisfying relationship which transcends their differences—except on a purely physical basis. This also holds true in reverse; it is the rare foreigner who can overcome his own attitudes, values, rules and other social instincts and replace them with a new set that requires him either to be bi-cultural or blot out his own personality.

The Japanese are programmed, by a deep desire to make a favorable impression, to give every indication that they wholeheartedly enjoy intercourse with foreigners. At the same time, they are also conditioned to abhor contact with outsiders and to look upon them as dangerous competitors if not outright enemies. This provides for a strange paradox. They crave to be like and admired, but from a distance. They are repelled by the thought of intimacy with a foreigner and yet force themselves to go through the motion . . . and once having done so consider themselves some kind of a martyr.

Thus for the Westerner to function smoothly in a Japanese business setting requires an extraordinary amount of subtlety, even a 6th sense, to maintain the delicate balance between ambiguity and the concrete, the suggestive and the direct and decisive. Probably the biggest danger in any such setting is the tendency of the foreigner to say too much, thus compounding the possibility for error or friction. In fact, one of the biggest mistakes many American businessmen make in their dealings with the Japanese is talking too much, over-stating their case. There is a tendency for the Japanese to assume that anyone who talks a lot and repeats himself in an effort to make a point, is insincere and possibly trying to pull a fast one.

The Japanese business system works less on cold objectivity, and more on emotion. In virtually all confrontations, the appeal that usually wins in the end is the emotional one—for harmony, for face, for the future benefit of the majority, etc. Emotion is the glue that binds the Japanese system together. If you want to get along with, influence, or lead a Japanese employee, associate or client, see to his emotional needs first.

Mōretsu-Shain
The "Gung-Ho" Employees

Although Japan had emerged as one of the top manufacturing nations of the world by 1960, it was not until the 1970s that the Japanese really hit their stride as salesmen. This has to be explained and qualified.

Selling, especially in the positive, aggressive manner practiced by Americans and some Europeans, is diametrically opposed to several of the primary themes in traditional Japanese culture. In "Japanese" behavior, a forward, aggressive approach was forbidden. The Japanese were taught, and quite literally forced, to be reticent, self-effacing, to speak in vague terms, to avoid bragging, to deprecate themselves and their belongings, and to be repelled by the opposite kind of behavior.

During the long centuries before Japan began doing business with the West, the only type of salesman known was the peddler or barker. Then, following industrialization, new methods of doing business which would have resulted in the need for salesmen did not develop. Japan became a nation of neighborhood shopkeepers and a few giant monopolies. It was not until about 1950 that Japanese companies began paying attention to their sales departments. As late as the mid-1950s, it was the worst kind of insult to suggest to a college graduate that he become a salesman. It was like seriously suggesting to a Yale or Harvard man that he get himself a shoeshine box and go to work on the sidewalks.

During the 1950s and early 1960s salesmanship in Japan also suffered because the average young employee placed in the sales or export department of his company had no "feel" for the merchandise he was supposed to sell. Not knowing his products intimately and in many cases not even being familiar with the way they were used, the manufacturer-exporter was at a considerable disadvantage when he attempted to sell to Westerners on anything other than a price basis. He was also handicapped by not knowing the psychology of the people he wanted to sell to, and by not wanting to make a mistake or be laughed at.

During the 1960s, several major Japanese companies ran elaborate television commercials designed to change the popular image of aggressive selling and sales people from negative to positive. At the same time, the young people coming of age during this period had not been conditioned to dislike or avoid aggressive behavior. Other consumer attitudes and habits were also changing during these years. By the mid 1970s, the Japanese style of "passive selling" had more or less been relegated to urban pockets of traditionalism and to isolated rural areas.

The popular image of the "new" Japanese that emerged in the late 1960s and early 70s was often described by the phrase *Mōretsu-shain* (Moe-ray-t'sue shah-een), or the "Gung-Ho" employee who works at top speed, and seemingly never relaxes. The connotation becomes clearer when you consider that *Mōretsu* literally means "fury" or "violence."

In international business, the Japanese are now sometimes criticized for "over selling," and for not being sensitive to the feelings of some of their potential customers, particularly in Southeast Asian countries. Now instead of being handicapped by poor salesmanship, or no salesmanship at all, the Japanese are handicapped by a general inability to deal effectively in cross-cultural relationships. They are acutely aware of the problem, however, and are carrying out educational and cross-cultural sensitization programs to help overcome it.

Chapter 8

Matome
Summing Up

Humanism Plus Authoritarianism

Generally speaking, Japan's management philosophy is based on a subtle balance of "humanism mixed with authoritarianism," and is patterned after the Japanese adaptation of an ideal Confucian family. In Confucian ethics, the ideal family is one that follows the *Five Principles:* Filial Piety, Fidelity, Obedience, Kindness and Loyalty to One's Superior.

When the Japanese imported Confucianism from China, they switched the order of the Five Principles, making loyalty to one's superior paramount, so the principles would fit in more readily with their own already existing authoritarian system.

Thereafter, the repression of one's own opinions and feelings, along with automatic submission to superior authority, was made second nature to the Japanese by the systematic application of intense physical and psychological pressures, backed up by swift punishment for anyone who resisted.

The authoritarian nature of this feudal family system of enterprise management was greatly tempered, however, by the broad application of a philosophy of humanism which had also been a traditional characteristic of the Japanese since ancient times. This humanism was a fundamental belief, *Shintō* in origin, that people should be selfless and kind, and help each other; that one who is in a superior position is morally obligated to take care of those who work for or serve him, and that peaceful harmony should be maintained by strict adherence to these beliefs.

The Parent-Child Ethic

Japan's distinctive humanism-plus-authoritarianism business system was translated into action in the form of a parent/child relationship. The employer was looked upon as a combination "mother and father," and the employees were his "children." Interpersonal relations between the two ideally followed the re-arranged Confucian principles, just as they were applied to private family life in Feudal Japan.

The particular strength of the typical large-scale Japanese company today springs from the traditional social manners and ethics as these were developed in the folds of the old feudal family system. For centuries, the people were taught to respect authority and to work cooperatively. In return for this, they were guaranteed a livelihood and protection. The system was held together and made to function smoothly by minutely defined personal obligations and a highly refined etiquette system. The focal points of the various controlling obligations were the central government, the clan, the family, and finally the individual.

The introduction of "individualism and democracy" into Japan in 1868 weakened and in some cases completely severed these feudalistic, obligatory ties. With the changeover to an industrial economy in the 1880s and 1890s the means of earning a living became the focal point in the lives of the Japanese. Company affiliation automatically replaced the clan, and to some extent the family as well, in the social fabric of the country. Businessmen inherited the loyalty, the respect and the service once given to the clan and the feudal government.

The development of modern industry in Japan thus was a primary factor in the breaking up of the feudal patterns in home life, but at the same time, the larger enterprises, especially, continued the functions of the old family and clan units, each company being a great family-clan of its own in which the traditional feudal patterns of obligation, loyalty and conduct have continued in only slightly diminished force.

The Western business executive who approaches a large Japanese company should therefore keep in mind that he is dealing with a "family" in which the members are ranked vertically according to their seniority and position, and that with only rare exceptions one member cannot commit the "family" to anything. The Japanese executive on whatever level must obtain the advice and consent of his "company relatives."

It must be recognized that the relationship between the larger Japanese employer and his employees is not strictly an economic one. The average employer gets from his workers a degree of loyalty, cooperation and effort that is seldom surpassed anywhere. In turn, the employer feels responsible not only for the economic welfare of his employees, but also takes an interest in their social and spiritual well-being.

This feeling of mutual obligation is repeated on every level of Japanese company management, with each responsible person doing his best to take care of those under him. The higher a person rises in management, the stronger this feeling tends to become. The more successful a Japanese businessman, the more generous he tends to become and the more he tries to do for his "family."

The distinctive Japanese family-company system is changing fairly rapidly under pressure from uncontrollable economic factors, but enough of it still remains to give Japanese companies and Japanese company management a special character of their own.

"Marine Corps" Management

One of the best ways to gain a quick "surface" insight into Japanese management philosophy and practices is to relate each company or organization to a military unit, particularly to the Marine Corps, operating under the "old book" of strict discipline in which rank is the foundation of all relationships.

Under this system every "enlistment" in a major Japanese corporation is in principle for the working life of the individual. Those with grade school and high school educations start as privates and eventually may become non-commissioned officers (blue-collar workers and foremen). All university graduates automatically become officer candidates (management trainees) when they "enlist," and all expect to be promoted to successively higher officer ranks as they build up longevity.

Pay scales are primarily based on longevity in service and rank, with promotions determined by time-in-grade, schooling, and other qualifications. The company lapel button is the "uniform" and the title on the name-card denotes rank. The *ojigi* or bow is the equivalent of the military salute. Inferiors are expected to pay proper respect to superiors, and to obey them without question. Superiors are responsible for both the good and bad actions of their subordinates, and can win and keep their respect and support only by taking care of them.

Just as the outsider generally does not enter the Marine Corps as a sergeant or captain, the Japanese company requires, with still only a few exceptions, that its "non-commissioned" officers (blue collar foremen) and officers (managers) come up through the ranks—and thus have a proper understanding and appreciation for the required manners and ethics.

Just as the different branches of the armed forces tend to compete with each other for everything from funds and research projects to women, so do Japanese companies. Within Japanese companies there is also the same sectional and departmental rivalry that was traditionally promoted in every military organization, from squads of foot-soldiers up to armies.

Activities within sections and departments in Japanese companies are very much like those in a squad, platoon or company of Marines, with similar attitudes toward responsibility and loyalty to their branch of service.

Just as military personnel are generally promoted to higher ranks according to their educational background (high school, university, academy, etc.), they also concern themselves with dates of promotion so that within the rank of captain, for example, Captain Smith outranks Captain Jones because Smith was promoted first and therefore has more time-in-grade.

Just as a well-trained and highly motivated squad of marines can naturally be expected to do well in battle, a Japanese group does particularly well in situations demanding close, cooperative team work. As in the military, the independent spirit or the innovator fares well in Japan only if he is capable of working within his group, foregoing personal ambitions and recognition.

Again, a primary advantage of the Japanese system of vertically ranking each individual and each group, and the various rules that govern the system, is that it can be galvanized for almost instant action, and can automatically be expected to perform like a well-drilled infantry squad. Each team member is responsible not only for his own but also his teammate's livelihood, and regardless of how he personally feels about the people he works with or what he is charged with doing, he is under extraordinary pressure to do his best.

The Emotional/Sensual Element

Despite the cultural idiosyncrasies that make Japanese and Western businessmen so different in attitudes, manners and methods, most Westerners who have been to Japan—and especially the men—are very strongly attracted by life among the Japanese.

This attraction is emotional and may be generalized into two categories, the "intellectual" and the sexual. Both of these areas are important, but the influence of the latter is often the strongest and certainly the most obvious.

There are two sides—and several facets—to the intellectual/emotional category. One side is the very strong sense of superiority that Westerners still feel toward Japanese. Because of racial and cultural prejudices, the average Westerner, living or traveling in Japan, is able to delude himself into believing he is better than even the most accomplished, wealthy or famous Japanese, regardless of their character or learning.

The other side of the intellectual category, which attracts all foreigners to varying degrees, including the most stupid ones, is that which appeals both consciously and subconsciously to their aesthetic sense, and to their admiration—from a distance—of some of the more benign aspects of Japan's unique civilization. Things Japanese that, in their own contexts, are pleasing to foreigners include traditional wearing apparel, handicrafts, architecture, landscape gardening and the rigid formality of Japanese etiquette.

There is also a very strong sense of the exotic surrounding everything that is typical of Old Japan, and this added dash of the romantic and mysterious contributes to the aesthetic pleasure experienced by foreigners confronted with a traditional Japanese scene.

The sexual category pertains almost entirely to men, and applies especially to those who were steeped in the Puritan-Christian concept that sex is basically sinful, and that monogamy and/or abstinence are moral virtues.

In Japan, sex has never had the stigma of evil. On the contrary it has always been considered an important part of living, playing a vital role in the native religion of the country, as well as having been sanctioned as a pleasure.

There were traditionally different sexual moralities for men and women in Japan, however. Generally, all men considered that they had a right to unconcealed sexual promiscuity, the volume and variety depending only upon what each individual could afford. Women, on the other hand, were divided into two groups: those who were known as "public women"—which included prostitutes and usually girls and women who worked in tea houses, inns and other eating and drinking places—and, non-working wives and their daughters—the famous O'josan (Oh-joe-sahn), who were brought up under very strict conditions and were usually, of course, the daughters of the better-to-do.

The O'josan and the wives of the privileged warrior class, and in particular the nobility, were not ascetics, however. Throughout most of Japan's history, they engaged in love affairs whenever possible, and were not subject to pangs of moral guilt or criticism stemming from a belief that virginity or marital faithfulness was a divine virtue. About the only difference between the public and "private" women of Japan, as far as their attitude toward sexual morality was concerned, was time, place and partner.

In Old Japan, especially lower class women, which included a big majority, but women of rank as well, were pretty much at the mercy of the proud, haughty Samurai who carried their male prerogative as far as their audacity and means would allow. The great chain of over 75,000 travelers' inns that flourished during the long Tokugawa era (from 1603 to 1868) functioned as nightly "love-tels." Legal and illegal redlight districts also flourished until *April Fool's Day*, 1956.

In Japan today the situation is pretty much the same as far as volume and variety of sexual activities are concerned. There are no concentrated, marked pleasure quarters, but there are more "public" girls, and the pampered daughter of the well-to-do is more apt to be abroad at night than the less fortunate girl who works in some office or store.

Since Japanese men tend to be as sexually active as their financial position allows and their inclinations dictate, it takes a large number of women partners to keep up with the demand. Most of these are provided by the famous *mizu shōbai* or entertainment trades—bars, cabarets, night clubs, Turkish bath houses, geisha houses, etc.,—which employ several hundred thousand girls and women.

In addition to the one-time liaisons between customers of these business establishments and their female employees, there is also wide-spread sexual activity among couples in the business and social world who become acquainted, then date. This includes older married men, who are usually in a much better financial position to carry on an outside affair because of their higher income brackets.

Most of the non-*mizu shōbai* women concerned are single, but it is not unusual for married women to have occasional or full-time lovers—especially since a significant percentage of their husbands not only carry on extra-marital affairs but also often spends nights away from home on company business.

There are thousands of small inn-hotels throughout Japan that exist by renting rooms—and bath if desired—to couples who use them for only an hour or so. Most of the famous resort areas like Atami and Ito depend to a considerable extent upon the weekend patronage of trysting couples to keep them flourishing. These very common weekend trips are often referred to—by the men, at least—as "weekend honeymoons," and the men who go on them regularly, with different girls as often as possible, refer to their partners as "weekend brides."

I have known a number of men who boasted they had had a different "weekend bride" almost every weekend for a period of several years.

Not having a sense of guilt about indulging in sex, the Japanese look at it in an entirely different light than what has been traditional among "Christianized" Westerners. At the same time, the idea that a girl who is not a virgin has endangered her chances of making a good marriage has been present in Japan since ancient times. It seems, however, that this belief is not nearly strong enough to counterbalance the other attitudes toward sex—one of which, in several parts of Japan, included "trial" marriages by couples who were attracted to each other. The boy and girl lived together, usually in the girl's home, for a few weeks or months to find out if they could get along. If they couldn't, and the girl wasn't pregnant, the boy returned home and started looking elsewhere.

It should not be surprising, therefore, that when the average Westerner finds himself in a society that still condones—in practice if no longer in principle—sexual promiscuity, he is apt to take to it like a duck to water. Some, in fact, go overboard. They are not content with a more or less full-time mistress or the occasional "short-time." They work at it systematically and take great pride in their "conquests." Two upstanding Americans I know once engaged in a contest to see which one could run up the longest string of free conquests in the shortest period of time. The winner had managed 64—in a few days under three months—when a serious case of strain called a halt to the race. The loser had marked up 47.

Another foreigner (from Germany), who came to Japan on a cultural exchange-student arrangement, spent his entire stay of one year trying to seduce school-girl virgins, and according to his own account, succeeded admirably.

In addition to the attraction provided by actual sexual contact, there is a sensualness and sexuality pervading Japanese culture that gives off a constant promise of sex. This promise is a powerful stimulant to the average Westerner, and it is the appeal of this distinctive atmosphere that holds many outsiders to Japan, rather than actual pleasures of the flesh.

Of course, much of the appeal of this sexual promise is provided by the Westerner's imagination. But there are in truth a number of qualities or characteristics possessed by most Japanese women—besides their general availability—that (when in a Japanese setting) give them definite advantages over the Western girl and often make this promise a reality. These include many of the qualities traditionally considered ideal in women by sexist-minded men.

Lafcadio Hearn, the original Japanophile—who later, after he had had time to really see behind the "Japanese mask," severely criticized Japan's social system—said that foreigners were attracted to (turn-of-the-century) Japan because it was like living in an illusion of some future paradise. He said this illusion of paradise was provided by the etiquette cult of the Japanese, which on the surface presented a picture of perfect harmony. There were also the old ideals of *Shintōism*, which included instinctive unselfishness, a universal sense of moral beauty, and a common desire to find joy in life by making happiness for others.

The Kindness Syndrome

For every example of a "bad" or "obnoxious" habit or manner that the Japanese have (from the Western viewpoint), a good or pleasing characteristic can also be pointed to, and it is obvious that the good side outweighs the bad. In over a decade of living and working in Japan, I had so many special kindnesses extended to me that at times it was actually embarrassing. Foreign visitors to Japan invariably have a number of such experiences with the Japanese that are genuine—and oftentimes startling—demonstrations of unselfish kindness.

My younger sister Rebecca, who visited Tokyo as a tourist, went off on her own one day to find the office of a steamship company. Since the addressing system in Tokyo (and most other Japanese cities) has nothing to do with the streets, most of which are not named, she became confused and ended up in the wrong section of downtown. Noticing her standing on a street corner looking perplexed, a man who couldn't speak English began trying to help her. When she was finally able to get the name of the Japanese steamship company across to him, he flagged a taxi and not only took her there but paid the fare.

Another very typical example: a friend forgot a pair of contact lenses in a taxi. She realized they were missing as soon as the taxi pulled way and tried to catch the driver's attention. He didn't see her frantic waving, but a young college student passerby did, and immediately went to her assistance. When he understood that she had left something in the cab, he escorted her to a police box down the street.

There was no policeman on duty at the stand, so the good Samaritan stopped another passerby and explained the situation to him. The second passerby hailed a cab and took my friend to the district police station—altogether spending nearly an hour to help an utter stranger whom he couldn't talk to.

Such incidents, as the above implies, are common, and although the long-time foreign resident often takes them for granted, the newcomer is immensely impressed and enthusiastic in his praise for the Japanese.

This very strong human element, which is characteristic of the Japanese when they are in their own environment and at peace with themselves and others, helps make living and working in Japan not only tolerable but a little more often than not, more satisfying than living "back home."

Sources of Japan's Strength

In addition to the human element that cancels out many of the attitudes and habits of the Japanese that are negative and disadvantageous, there are other factors, psychological and sociological, that explain why the Japanese, despite their failings, are a formidable race and why Japan is one of the world's top industrial powers.

The first and most important of these factors has been the willingness of the Japanese to sacrifice. From earliest times the Japanese were taught and conditioned to believe that it was a virtue to devote their labor and lives to fulfill the various obligations that were the essence of their society.

This willingness to sacrifice has been the one prevailing ethic by which the people lived through the centuries and which made possible the development of all the various attitudes and habits that distinguish the Japanese from other people. Until the coming of economic affluence in the 1960s, it was visible in every aspect of their society.

Along with this willingness to sacrifice came a willingness to be regimented and homogenized. The Japanese became alike mentally and socially to such an extent that they more or less functioned as a single unit; one giant family with a common head. The secret of the nation's rise to the heady heights of a world power is simply that most everybody worked together for the same end for considerably less personal benefit than workers in other industrialized countries.

Another factor that also tempers to a great extent the more harsh aspects of Japanese society and at the same time contributes to the industrial prowess of Japan, is the very deep and broad stream of aestheticism permeating the traditional culture.

This stream of aestheticism was so deeply intertwined within the traditional life-style of the Japanese that it was a part of their cultural inheritance; something they learned and applied as part of their being Japanese. Until as late as the 1950s, the Japanese seemed to inherit not only a sense of but a desire for harmony in all things—in their selection of colors, architecture, handicrafts, apparel lines, dimensions, speech and actions, including such violent ones as suicide.

Factors that played leading roles in the development of an aesthetic civilization in Japan include the powerful influence of *Shintō* and *Zen Buddhism*, the capsule size of the country, the remarkable homogeneity of the people, the all-powerful *Confucian*-oriented feudal government under which the Japanese lived for so many centuries; and long before this, some peculiar trait in the people that seems to always have been present.

One of the most interesting of these influences was *Zen Buddhism*, as manifested in the tea ceremony, still widely practiced in Japan. To those with only a cursory knowledge of Japan and the Japanese, ascribing to the familiar but little understood tea ceremony anything more than "tea with some rules" may sound farfetched, but to declare that the tea ceremony is one of the principal manifestations for much that is called "Japanese" may sound strange indeed. Nevertheless, it is so.

The tea ceremony as practiced by the Japanese is essentially a worship of the natural, and an attempt to achieve perfect harmony with themselves and with nature. The tea room, the most important accessory in the tea ceremony, is a different world; free from all vulgarity; free from the slightest distraction, so that one can surrender himself completely to the adoration of natural beauty, to striving for physical and spiritual union.

It is unfortunate that this ceremony has not been better explained by the Japanese or better understood in the West, for what most foreigners regard as a simple demonstration of a Japanese idiosyncracy (the results of which is a bitter, "practically undrinkable" tea), is in reality the first time—and perhaps the last time—that man has made into a cult the unselfish appreciation of simple, natural beauty.

As a result of the remarkable aesthetic sense of the Japanese, there was traditionally a subtle charm and in many instances an exquisite beauty in the basic form and decorative design of native Japanese products. It is this distinctive charm and beauty, called *shibui* in Japanese, that captured the imagination of the Western world when Japan first became known to the West.

The aesthetic theme is still conspicuous in Japan today, although there is a tremendous gap between the attitudes and practices of people born after 1945 and those who are older. The theme is obviously weakening under the onslaught of Western products and ideas, but it is still there in the language, architecture, crafts and the remnants of the traditional life-style. It still provides the Japanese of all ages with an unique source of strength and satisfaction that is sorely lacking in other industrial societies.

Pride, Prejudice & Perseverance

The Japanese have always been a fantastically proud and—given the opportunity—ambitious people. This pride and burning ambition to prove their superiority, or at least their equality, accounts for a great deal of their strength, energy and perseverance. They are constantly measuring their accomplishments against the world's best or the world's largest. The more successful they are, the more convinced they become that their way is the right way.

The fact that Japan has been amazingly successful in recent decades has convinced most older Japanese businessmen that their business system, which is an outgrowth of their national character, is the best in the world. Japanese businessmen admire the efficiency of the American system, but they are critical of it because to them it is "inhuman" and debasing. They are quick to point out that American management techniques do not "fit" the character and preference of the Japanese.

The Japanese are, in fact, virtually obsessed with their "National Character," and spend a great deal of time and money studying it. These studies show that the Japanese generally consider themselves happy and contented, and that they regard themselves as the hardest working, the most diligent, politest, kindest and most patient people in the world. The typical Japanese businessman is always very much concerned about upholding the honor of Japan and the Japanese in any dealings with outsiders. In his own mind, he never acts alone. He is acting for and under the scrutiny of one hundred million-plus fellow Japanese.

It is still typical of Japanese businessmen to assume a humble attitude in the presence of visitors. This often gives the resident or visiting Western businessman a high feeling of superiority—and frequently leads him to underestimate the Japanese and to commit excesses. The Japanese businessman is simply being polite and treating the foreigner as an honored guest.

Virtually all management personnel in larger Japanese companies are university graduates, and regard themselves as an elite group and as intellectuals. It is also characteristic of those who have gone into the government ministries to harbor a certain amount of cultural, racial and political resistance against the world-at-large, and to regard themselves as Japan's first bulwark of defense against "excessive" foreign business encroachment. They are not adverse, however, to learning all they can from outsiders and adapting the knowledge to their own advantage.

The Japanese executive is deeply committed to the management system in his own company because, in the ways that count, his company is his life. The penalty for not conforming, for breaking the traditional pattern, is very serious. If he should step out of line he is either shunted aside or ostracized—and unless he has very powerful family connections, he has practically no chance of being taken in by another company of comparable standing.

Individually, the Japanese businessman is not bound by immutable principles of good, bad or logic in the American sense. He adapts easily and readily to suit the circumstances, and has a starkly realistic attitude toward power and what suits his (and Japan's) best interests. The old characteristics of abhorring selfishness and regarding profit-making as a social evil have long since been relegated to the background. His life is so closely tied in with the company and the company system that his own opinions seldom count for anything.

The Japanese businessman is usually a far more complex individual than his Western counterpart and, in a different way, is subjected to a great deal more stress. Once he enters a large company as a young man, he has very little direct control over his future. He must adhere to severely demanding etiquette and ethical codes in order to avoid upsetting the harmony of the system, knowing all the while that he will most likely spend his entire working life intimately linked to the same co-workers.

The Japanese management system is first of all geared to obtain maximum cooperation from employees with a minimum of friction, and only secondarily to obtaining business results. The fact that the system works extremely well is obvious.

Most Japanese executives support the system because they are so caught up in its web they must perpetuate it to survive. It is changing, however, though slowly and often imperceptibly, even in the old-line companies. These changes will accelerate as time goes on.

The Japanese are very much aware that many of their habits, customs and attitudes seriously handicap them in their international relations. In the early 1970s, leaders in business, government and education began saying that the Japanese may have to become *un-Japanese* if they are to really succeed, for the long haul, in the outside world.

This is a remarkable thing to contemplate, because they are talking about the very fabric of their culture: their language, their values, their attitudes and manners. The Japanese are, of course, changing and becoming less "Japanese"; but slowly. Too slowly, in the eyes of a growing number. In their view, among the several challenges now facing them is whether or not they can, in fact, change their national character fast enough and far enough to succeed in their goals.

Chapter 9

Glossary of Useful & Interesting Terms

Aisatsu (Aye-sot-sue)—Usually translated into English as "greeting" ("formal meeting" is more often correct, I think), the *aisatsu* has a great deal more significance in its Japanese context than "greeting" implies. The Japanese attach considerable importance to personally meeting and greeting, in a formalized way, personal as well as business contacts on certain special occasions.

There are two especially important *aisatsu* occasions in business in Japan. The first one is when you make your initial call on a company. The second one is when you visit companies with which you have established relations to express thanks for something special, to introduce an important member of your firm (your replacement, for example), to announce a new product, plan or affiliation, and at New Year's to demonstrate gratitude for past business and your sincere desire to continue the relationship in the future.

The first personal contact between two companies in Japan can be a vital factor in subsequent relations, so it is important that it be done properly. The more important the proposed relationship, the higher ranking the participants in the *aisatsu* should be. A major tie-up calls for a meeting between the presidents of the two firms. This, traditionally, is just a get-acquainted meeting. Specific details of the association are not discussed. The prime function of the high-level *aisatsu* is to put the official seal of approval on the new relationship so that subordinate executives thereafter can proceed to develop the association in confidence.

Antei (Ahn-tay-ee)—The sense of security/care Japanese workers expect to get from their employment.

Base-up—An expression used (mostly) by unions in reference to their annual spring drive to win increases in the base wages of workers.

Bessō (Base-so)—A villa, usually in the mountains or on the sea-coast, originally for recreational or retirement purposes of the well-to-do. Now, most *bessō* in Japan are owned by companies and used by employees as a fringe benefit.

Buchō dairi (Boo-choe die-ree)—*Dairi* means "agent," "deputy," or "assistant." A *buchō dairi* is therefore an assistant department head. A *kachō dairi* is a deputy section chief, etc.

Chōchin kiji (Choe-cheen key-jee)—A *chochin* is a paper lantern, and a *kiji* is a newspaper or magazine article. A "*chochin kiji*" is a story that "sheds light" on some company product or topic, and refers to "news" articles accompanying advertisements, usually on the same page or at least in the same section of the publication as the ad. The Japanese version of a "puff article."

Danshi jūgyō-in (Dhan-she jew-ghee-yoe-een)—All male employees below the rank of *kachō* (section head).

Dorai (Doe-rye)—This is the English word "dry." The Japanese adopted it to mean the kind of impersonal, profit-oriented approach to business attributed to Western businessmen. Conversely, their own *ninjō* (human feelings) oriented business system is regarded as "wet" ("wetto"). The same words are also applied to one's attitude toward the opposite sex.

Dōsatsu ryoku (Doe-sot-sue ree-yoe-coo)—Able to "see through things," to have "keen insight;" a quality the Japanese look for in a top executive.

Fuku shachō (Foo-coo shah-choe)—A *fuku shachō* is a "vice president"—a rank that is not as common in Japan as in the West. In Japanese companies, the role of the vice president is more likely filled by a director.

Fundoshi hitotsu de (Foon-doe-she he-tote-sue day)—Literally, "with one 'fundoshi'." A *fundoshi* is a narrow loin cloth, and is the traditional Japanese equivalent of "shorts" or "panties" as the case may be. The phrase *"fundoshi hitotsu de"* is an old one and refers to starting a company with little or no capital—on a "G-string" instead of a shoestring.

Gaijin (Guy-gene)—An "Outside Person," this is the Japanese word for "foreigner." You hear it often in Japan because foreigners there, especially caucasians, blacks and browns, stick out like sore thumbs. The connotation of the word has long been derogatory, so speakers often add the word *kata*, very polite for "person," to it—*gaijin-no kata* or "foreign person."

Gekokujo (Gay-coe-coo-joe)—To go over the head of one's superior, something that in Feudal Days could result in one losing his own, literally. The practice is still very much frowned on in contemporary Japan, and frequently acts as a barrier to business.

Gote-ni mawaru (Go-tay-nee ma-wah-rue)—Also derived from the game of *Go*, this figuratively means to get behind or be behind. In a business context it refers to letting your competitor or negotiating counterpart get one up on you.

Gyōsei-shidō (Ghee-yoe-say-she-doe)—This is the famous (or infamous) "Administrative Guidance" of business practiced by bureaucrats in several key government Ministries. The "guidance" consists of forcing or persuading businessmen to follow certain policies or guidelines that are not required by law but are believed by the bureaucrats to be in the interest of the country. The pressure the Ministries can bring to bear on individual companies as well as industries is enormous, and not very many businessmen can successfully resist *gyōsei-shidō*.

Hara-gei (Hah-rah-gay-ee)—"Stomach art," a method of doing business that depends on "gut feeling" and is often characterized as being subtle, devious and/or cunning. The word is not heard very often any more, but the practice is still common.

Hito hada nugu (He-toe hah-dah new-goo)—Literally, "to remove one layer of skin." Figuratively, to do someone a favor without expecting anything in return; or to repay a past favor.

Honne to tatemae (Hone-nay toe tah-tay-my)—Over the centuries, the Japanese were conditioned to avoid direct statements and any behavior that might result in friction, responsibility, etc. They thus became expert at "reading between the lines" when presented with only the "framework" *(tatemae)* of one's "thoughts" *(honne)*. This manner of speaking and behaving is still characteristic of un-Westernized Japanese.

Isekki-mōkeru (Eesay-key moe-kay-rue)—To take someone to a bar, restaurant, geisha house, etc., in order to get on friendly terms prior to discussing business. The word is archaic, but the practice is very up-to-date.

Joshi jūgyō-in (Joe-she jew-ghee-yoe-een)—All female employees in a company.

Kaigi (Kie-ghee)—A meeting, or conference, of which there are many kinds in Japan. In their meetings, particularly for the purpose of negotiating business arrangements, the Japanese seem to be most comfortable with a group made up of about 10 persons, with each allowed to have his say. Such meetings most often start out in a relaxed, informal way. Their custom of discussing every possibility often results in talks going on for days to weeks—and sometimes for months.

Kanryō shugi (Khan-rio shoe-ghee)—A term referring to the manners and attitudes associated with bureaucrats, i.e. bureaucratic.

Kenami ga yoi (Kay-nah-me gah-yoe-ee)—Literally, "good stock," as a dog or horse with good blood-lines; but also frequently used in reference to a person with a good family and educational background.

Kessai-ken (Kayce-sie-ken)—This is the authority under which a ranking executive approves of a *ringi-sho* proposal, thereby permitting his subordinates to take whatever action the document calls for. Approving a *ringi-sho* under the *kessai-ken* does not mean, however, that the ranking executive is responsible for the results of the policy or project if it fails.

Kone (Cone-nay)—Short for "connections" or "personal connections"; through family or school ties, etc. A very important asset in Japan's business world.

Meibutsu (May-ee-boo-t'sue)—"Famous product." Practically every region or prefecture in Japan has been noted for one or more particular products for centuries. Always popular with travelers, some are now distributed nationally. Also: *Meibutsu otoko* (oh-toe-coe), or "outstanding man."

Meiwaku (May-ee-wah-coo)—An "apology." Literally, the word means "trouble," or "annoyance," etc. In Japan the formal apology generally includes humiliating one's self, accepting responsibility, and often restitution in the form of cash payments for damages, mental suffering, sickness, etc.

Mekura-ban (May-coo-rah-bahn)—By itself, *mekura* means "blind." *Ban* means "watchman" or "guard." Put together they refer to an executive stamping his name-seal on a *ringi-sho* without reading it.

Naikei (Nie-kay-ee)—"Unwritten rules," usually referring to various practices followed by lower ranking bureaucrats in the Ministry of International Trade and Industry and the Finance Ministry, which often go beyond the laws regulating these two agencies.

Natsuin (Not-sue-een)—This is the formal word for the name-seal or "stamp" *(hanko)* still widely used in Japan instead of signatures.

Nenkin seido (Nane-keen say-ee-doe)—"Pension system," something that is of growing importance to Japanese workers.

Onjin (Own-gene)—"Obligation Person," or a person who helps another in some important area like getting into a choice school or company. The *onjin* is thereafter "responsible" for the person helped, and may act as a go-between in matters relating to him or her. The obligation felt by the person receiving the help lasts for a life-time.

O'rei (Oh-ray-ee)—The etiquette that requires all debts and favors be acknowledged and paid for by bowing, expressing thanks or gratitude, giving gifts, etc.

Otoko ga tatanai (Oh-toe-coe-gah tah-tah-nie)—"My manhood won't stand up!" This is a phrase often used by a man (usually young) when pleading that he be allowed to assume a certain responsibility, or be given a certain task, for the sake of his "manly honor."

Senjitsu wa dōmo arigatō gozaimasu (Sane-jee-t'sue wah do-moe ah-ree-gah-toe go-zie-mah-sue)—This is another of those institutionalized phrases, ritualistically repeated, that plays a key role in Japanese manners and ethics. It means, "Thank you for the other day," and is said the next time you meet your benefactor after you have been treated to a dinner and/or night out on the town. By repeating this phrase, you acknowledge that you are indebted to your host for his hospitality, and expect to reciprocate in the future (not necessarily by taking him out). If any "understanding" was achieved during the dinner or drinking bout that followed, this is also the standard phrase used to express gratitude.

Sen-te wo utsu (Sane-tay oh ooh-t'sue)—Derived from the Japanese game of *Go*, which is similar to chess and very popular with businessmen, this phrase means to make a move that forces an opponent into an untenable position where he has to move in your favor. It has the connotation of "being ahead of the game," and is used in reference to business negotiations and other situations.

GLOSSARY OF USEFUL & INTERESTING TERMS 157

Shita-uke (She-tah-ou-kay)—A small factory that depends for all or a major part of its business on sub-contracts from larger companies.

Shonen-kyū (Show-nane-que)—Starting salary for new employees. Literally, "first-year-income," which is based on educational level and size of the company.

Shukkō (Shuke-coe)—Literally, "to leave" or "depart," *shukko* is used in business to mean "transfer," and refers specifically to a company transferring personnel to related firms—to get rid of them; to exercise direct control over the firms; to strengthen its ties with the companies; to provide young managerial candidates with additional training.

Shumu kisoku (Shoe-moo key-so-coo)—These are "rules of employment," something most Japanese workers have to read and sign when first hired.

Sode-no shita (So-day-no she-tah)—Literally, "under the kimono sleeve." A bribe, usually thought of in connection with bureaucrats, who used to be most prone to require such "special consideration" before they would move. The phrase is old, but the practice is still popular, usually taking the form of parties, expense-paid trips and other services-in-kind.

Soroban to awanai (So-roe-bahn toe ah-wah-nie)—Another old term that is good for a laugh. It was used to indicate that a price was too high, or a business proposition would not be profitable. Its literal meaning is "It doesn't agree with the abacus."

Tatakidai (Tah-tah-key-die)—*Tatakidai* literally means "a platform for pounding." It is used in business contexts to mean a suggestion or plan proposed by a lower ranking manager as a starting point for group discussions by all company executives concerned. If a consensus is reached, the plan may be adopted. The equivalent, you might say, of a "verbal *ringi-sho*."

Tsugo ga warui-no de (T'sue-go gah wah-roo-ee-no day) —"Because of an inconvenience . . ." This is the most common excuse given for declining to go somewhere or do something when the individual doesn't want to or cannot for some reason. No other explanation is given or asked for.

Uka kosaku (Ooh-cah coe-sah-coo)—To "fix" something behind the scenes; often applicable when one is petitioning the government for something, or is negotiating a business deal.

Wakarimashita (Wah-cah-ree-mah-she-tah)—This is the past-tense of *wakarimasu*, which means "to understand." When Japanese businessmen (and politicians) say "*wakarimashita*," it sometimes means "I understand . . . but." It's the unspoken "but" that you have to watch out for, because this particular "I understand" doesn't mean the person is going to do anything about whatever is understood.

Yakutsuki (Yah-coo-t'sue-key)—Literally "with title," this word refers to a person who has a title, and is therefore a manager or executive. Anyone above the *sha-in* level.

Yoroshiku (Yoe-row-she-coo)—One of the most frequently used words in the Japanese language, this means "Please do something for me (or us)!" It is used in a multitude of situations, with the meaning varying to fit whatever situation is at hand. Its closest English equivalent is "Please do what you can (or all you can) for me," when you want the other party to do something for you that is quite important. The full, polite phrase is, *Yoroshiku onegai itashimasu* (Yoe-row-she-coo oh-nay-guy ee-tah-she-mah-sue).

Yūryokusha (You-ree-yoe-coo-shah)—"A person with influence," or someone who has enough pull to get the son or daughter of a friend or relative a job in a desirable company, etc.

Zaibatsu (Zie-baht-sue)—"Financial clique," or a large industrial combine, often monopolistic in practice if not in principle. Ten or so of Japan's largest *zaibatsu* control over 50 percent of the country's business.

Zaikai-jin (Zie-kie-gene)—*Zaikai* means something like "high finance" or "financial circles," and *jin* means "person." Combined, the two refer to a distinguished, generally wealthy, senior man, often retired from the highest levels of business or finance, who acts as a neutral counselor for major firms or groups involved in important deals. A variation of this term also used in reference to these high-level go-betweens is *Zaikai-shidosha* (she-doe-shah). *Shidosha* means "leader" or "expert."